Cybersecurity Architecture Fundamentals

Ian Loe

Copyright © 2024 by Ian Loe

All rights reserved.

No portion of this book may be reproduced in any form without written permission from the publisher or author, except as permitted by U.S. copyright law.

This publication is designed to provide accurate and authoritative information in regard to the subject matter covered. It is sold with the understanding that neither the author nor the publisher is engaged in rendering legal, investment, accounting or other professional services. While the publisher and author have used their best efforts in preparing this book, they make no representations or warranties with respect to the accuracy or completeness of the contents of this book and specifically disclaim any implied warranties of merchantability or fitness for a particular purpose. No warranty may be created or extended by sales representatives or written sales materials. The advice and strategies contained herein may not be suitable for your situation. You should consult with a professional when appropriate. Neither the publisher nor the author shall be liable for any loss of profit or any other commercial damages, including but not limited to special, incidental, consequential, personal, or other damages.

First edition 2024

To all those who have contributed to my journey of learning and growth,

This book is dedicated to you.

Thank you for sharing your knowledge, insights, and experiences with me over the years. Each interaction, conversation, and lesson has been a stepping stone in my quest for understanding and enlightenment.

To the mentors who have guided me, the teachers who have inspired me, and the colleagues who have collaborated with me, your wisdom has shaped my perspective and fueled my curiosity.

To the authors whose words have enlightened me, the researchers whose discoveries have fascinated me, and the thinkers whose ideas have challenged me, your contributions have enriched my mind and expanded my horizons.

To my friends and family who have supported me, encouraged me, and believed in me, your love and encouragement have sustained me through the highs and lows of this journey.

This book is a testament to the collective wisdom of all those who have crossed my path, leaving an indelible mark on my intellect and spirit.

Thank you for being part of my lifelong pursuit of knowledge.

Content

Introduction to Cybersecurity 1
  Security Operations Domain 2
    Network Security 2
    Cloud Security 2
    Endpoint Security 3
    Identity and Access Management (IAM) 3
    Disaster Recovery and Business Continuity 3
    Data Loss Prevention (DLP) 3
    Operational Security (OpSec) 4
    Cyber-Physical Systems Security 4
    Information Security 4
      Encryption 4
    Threat Intelligence 5
    Cybersecurity Architecture 5
    Application Security 6
      Security in DevSecOps 6
    Governance, Risk Management, and Compliance (GRC) 7
      Governance 8
      Risk Management 8
      Compliance 8

Threat Modeling 10
  Why security requirements are hard 12
  What are the various threat modeling views 14
  Various Models of Threat Modeling 15
    STRIDE 15
    DREAD 17
    PASTA 19
    TRIKE 22
    VAST (Visual, Agile, and Simple Threat Modeling) 25
    Attack Trees 29
    LINDDUN 32
    OCTAVE 34
    CVSS (Common Vulnerability Scoring System) 36
    MITRE ATT&CK Framework 39
    Persona non Grata 42

Threat Modeling Views 44
  Functional View 44

Deployment View	47
Data Flow View	50
Environmental View	53
Social View	55

A Threat Modeling Example — 59

Enterprise Security Technologies — 63

Network Security	66
Network Security Tools	67
Firewalls	67
Intrusion Detection/Prevention Systems	70
Network Access Control (NAC)	72
Packet Capture Tools	75
Network Visibility Tools	79
Security Policy Enforcement	81
Real-Time Technology Enforcement	81
Passive Technology-Assisted Compliance Check	82
Non-Technical Compliance Check	83
Contractual Compliance Check	84
Endpoint Security	85
Basic Endpoint Protection	85
Advanced Endpoint Protection	87
Next Generation Endpoint Protection	88
The Cyber Kill Chain	89
Identity and Access Management	92
IAM Tools	93
Identity Management	94
Access Management	95
Difference between IAM and IGA	95
Application Security	97
Code Security	98
System Security	98
Availability	100
Database Security	101
Operating Systems Security	103
Cloud-Native Security	105
Data Protection	109
Vulnerability and Patch Management	114
Availability Management	118
Supply Chain Security	120
Security Operations Center (SOC)	123
SIEM (Security Information and Event Management)	123

SOAR (Security Orchestration, Automation, and Response)	123
Next-Generation Platforms	124
Integration in Enterprise Security Architecture	124
Mobile Device Security	126
Mobile Device Management (MDM)	128
Mobile Application Management (MAM)	128
Sandboxing	128
Self-Destruction of Data	129

Cloud Security   130

Key Cloud Security Concepts	132
Log Frequency and Timeliness	132
Privileged User Management	133
Secrets/Keys Management	133
Cloud Security Architecture Areas	134
Cloud Infrastructure Scope	134
Network Security	136
Virtual Private Cloud (VPC)	136
Network Gateways	137
Load Balancers	139
Network Segmentation	141
VPC Peering	143
Site-to-Site VPN	145
VPC Endpoints	145
Network Security Services	146
Compute Security	149
Virtual Machines (VMs)	149
Containers and Kubernetes Security	149
Serverless Computing Security	150
Cloud Tenancy	150
Microservice Security	151
Storage Security	152
Virtual Disk	152
Object Storage	152
File Storage	153
Databases	153
General Security Considerations for Cloud Storage	153
Secrets Management	155
Types of Key Management	155
Key Rotation Practice	156
Cloud Identity and Access Management	158
Granular Access Control	158
Multi-Factor Authentication (MFA)	159

    Identity Federation and Single Sign-On (SSO) 159
    Auditing and Compliance Reporting 159
    Automated Provisioning and De-provisioning 160
  Cloud Logging and Monitoring 161
    Key Components and Practices 162
  Compliance and Security Best Practices 164
    Compliance in the Cloud 164
    Security Best Practices 165
  Continuous Compliance and Security Improvement 166

Cybersecurity Processes — 168

  Risk Management 170
  Risk Categories 170
  Risk Treatment 171
  Risk Assessment 172
    Risk Analysis 173
    Risk Mitigation 173
    Risk Monitoring 173
    Residual Risk 174
  Audit and Compliance 176
  Incident Response 178
    IR Frameworks 178

Architecture Documentation — 181

  Architecture Views 182
  Architecture Language 184
  Documenting a View 189
  Architecture Decisions Document (ADD) 191
    Examples of an ADD 194

Putting it All Together — 195

  Integration of Threat Models 195
  Technology Selection 196
  Architecture Diagrams in All Views 196
  Architecture Decision Documents 196

About The Author — 198

Introduction to Cybersecurity

According to the Federal Information Processing Standard (FIPS) (*The National Institute of Standards and Technology (NIST), 2010*) there are three security core principles that guide the information security area:

Confidentiality: preserve the access control and disclosure restrictions on information. Guarantee that no one will be break the rules of personal privacy and proprietary information.

Integrity: avoid the improper (unauthorized) information modification or destruction. Here is included ensure the non-repudiation and information authenticity.

Availability: the information must be available to access and use all the time and with reliable access. Certainly, it just must be true for those who have right of access.

These 3 principles are also called the "CIA Triad" and they serves as the cornerstone of security practices and helps organizations to design, implement, and maintain secure systems by balancing these three key objectives. By adhering to these principles, organizations can protect against a wide range of security threats and vulnerabilities, ensuring the protection and resilience of their information systems.

Cybersecurity Domains

Cybersecurity is a broad field that encompasses various domains aimed at protecting data, networks, devices, and programs from unauthorized access, attacks, or damage. Here's a breakdown of the primary domains and subdomains of cybersecurity:

Security Operations Domain

Under the domain of security operations, we look at how security in enforced in the running of the organization. Subdomains here includes:

Network Security

This subdomain focuses on protecting the network infrastructure and the data flowing within it from unauthorized access, misuse, malfunction, modification, destruction, or improper disclosure. Techniques include firewalls, intrusion detection systems (IDS), intrusion prevention systems (IPS), and virtual private networks (VPNs).

Cloud Security

With the increasing adoption of cloud computing, cloud security has become a crucial domain. It focuses on securing data stored online via cloud computing platforms from theft, leakage, and deletion. This includes the use of encryption, identity, and access management (IAM), and secure software interfaces.

Endpoint Security

Endpoint security aims to secure individual devices (endpoints) from malicious activities. As endpoints often serve as entry points for threats, this domain includes antivirus software, anti-spyware software, and firewall protection for laptops, desktops, and mobile devices.

Identity and Access Management (IAM)

IAM is a framework of policies and technologies ensuring that the right users (in an enterprise) have the appropriate access to technology resources. It involves the identification, authentication, and authorization of individuals to access systems, networks, and applications based on predefined roles and privileges.

Disaster Recovery and Business Continuity

This subdomain focuses on restoring data and operations with minimal downtime after a cybersecurity incident or other disruption. It includes planning for data backup, system recovery, and maintaining operations during and after a disaster.

Data Loss Prevention (DLP)

DLP involves strategies and tools to prevent data breaches, exfiltration, or unwanted destruction of sensitive information. Policies and technologies are used to classify critical information that cannot be disclosed and to prevent unauthorized access and transfer.

Operational Security (OpSec)

Operational security involves the processes and decisions for handling and protecting data assets. This includes the policies and procedures for protecting data in use and determining how and where to store or share data securely.

Cyber-Physical Systems Security

This subdomain addresses the security of physical systems that are controlled or monitored by computer-based algorithms, largely in the realm of critical infrastructure (power grid, water supply, etc.) and IoT devices. It involves protecting physical systems from cyber-attacks that could lead to physical damage.

Information Security

The next domain is Information Security, or InfoSec, which involves protecting the integrity and privacy of data, both in storage and in transit. This domain encompasses encryption, hashing, tokenization, and other methods to secure information against unauthorized access and leaks.

Encryption

Encryption is a foundational domain within cybersecurity, playing a critical role in protecting the confidentiality, integrity, and authenticity of information. It is the process of converting plaintext data into a coded form or ciphertext, making it unreadable to unauthorized users. Encryption relies on algorithms and cryptographic keys to secure data, ensuring that only those with the correct key can decrypt and access the original information. Encryption serves as a critical barrier against cyber threats, ensuring data privacy and security across various digital platforms and applications. Its role in cybersecurity will continue to evolve as technology advances and new challenges emerge, necessitating ongoing research and development to ensure robust protection against sophisticated attacks.

Threat Intelligence

Threat Intelligence is another domain within cybersecurity that focuses on collecting, analyzing, and disseminating information about existing or emerging threats and vulnerabilities that could potentially impact an organization's security posture. The primary goal of threat intelligence is to enable organizations to understand the risks of cyber-attacks and to make informed decisions on how to prepare, prevent, and respond to them effectively.

Cybersecurity Architecture

Cybersecurity architecture is a framework that specifies the organizational structure, processes, and technology designed to protect networked systems and data from breaches, attacks, or other threats. It serves as a blueprint for implementing effective security controls and measures that align with the organization's cybersecurity policies and risk management strategies. A well-designed cybersecurity architecture will encompass not only technical components but also processes and people, ensuring a comprehensive approach to safeguarding digital assets.

The goal of cybersecurity architecture is to create a secure environment for the organization's operations, protect against known and emerging threats, and comply with regulatory requirements, all while supporting the organization's strategic objectives.

Application Security

Application security is concerned with keeping software and devices free of threats. A compromised application could provide access to the data its designed to protect. This includes security considerations during the development stage, such as secure coding practices, and after deployment, such as patch management and application updates. A closely related subdomain to support this is DevSecOps.

Security in DevSecOps

Closely related to the domain of Application Security is DevSecOps, which integrates security practices within the DevOps process. DevOps, a combination of development and operations, emphasizes the rapid and continuous delivery of software. By integrating security as a core component of the software development lifecycle (SDLC), DevSecOps aims to ensure the creation of secure software without sacrificing speed and innovation. Key aspects of security in DevSecOps include:

Shift Left:Integrating security early in the SDLC, often summarized as "shifting left," means that security considerations and testing are introduced at the earliest stages of development. This approach helps in identifying and mitigating vulnerabilities early, reducing the cost and effort required to address them later.

Automation: DevSecOps relies heavily on automated tools to integrate security checks and testing throughout the development process. This includes static and dynamic analysis, dependency scanning, and automated compliance checks, ensuring that security assessments are performed consistently and efficiently.

Collaboration: DevSecOps fosters a culture of collaboration between development, operations, and security teams. By working together from the start, these teams can ensure that security is not an afterthought but a fundamental aspect of the development process.

Continuous Feedback: Continuous monitoring and feedback mechanisms are integral to DevSecOps. These practices help in the rapid identification of security issues and the implementation of corrective measures, thereby enhancing the security posture over time.

Security in DevSecOps represents a paradigm shift from traditional security approaches, where security was often a separate, final step before deployment. By making security an integral part of the development and deployment process, organizations can build and maintain more secure systems, reduce vulnerabilities, and adapt more quickly to changing security landscapes.

Governance, Risk Management, and Compliance (GRC)

GRC is a structured approach that aligns IT with business objectives, while effectively managing risk and meeting compliance requirements. In the context of cybersecurity, GRC is essential for establishing a strategic framework that ensures an organization's information technology systems are used and managed responsibly, risks are identified and mitigated, and regulatory and legal obligations are met. Let's break down the three components of GRC in the cybersecurity context:

Governance

Governance refers to the overall management approach through which senior executives direct and control the entire organization, using a combination of policies and procedures. In cybersecurity, governance involves setting clear priorities for the protection of data and systems, establishing cybersecurity policies, and ensuring that these policies are implemented effectively. It ensures that cybersecurity activities are aligned with the organization's goals and objectives, and that IT investments are rationalized to deliver the best value to the organization.

Risk Management

Risk Management in cybersecurity involves identifying, assessing, and taking steps to minimize the impact of risks to the organization's information assets. This includes threats such as cyber-attacks, data breaches, and other security incidents that could potentially harm the organization's operations, reputation, or bottom line. Risk management processes help in prioritizing risks based on their potential impact and likelihood, allowing organizations to focus their resources on the most significant threats and vulnerabilities, and implementing controls to mitigate these risks.

Compliance

Compliance involves adhering to laws, regulations, policies, and standards that apply to an organization's cybersecurity practices. This can include national and international cybersecurity standards, industry-specific regulations, and internal policies. The goal of compliance in the cybersecurity context is to ensure that the organization's data handling and security measures meet the required legal and regulatory standards, thereby protecting the organization from legal penalties, financial losses, and reputational damage.

This list is non-exhaustive, as technology evolves, some of these domains will also evolve to address new threats.

Threat Modeling

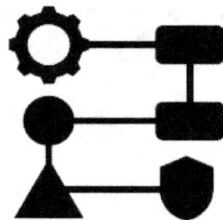

As we embark on the journey to learn how to design solutions to fortify our digital landscapes against a backdrop of ever-evolving cyber threats, it's crucial to begin with a cornerstone concept that sets the stage for all cybersecurity measures: Threat Modeling. This foundational chapter is dedicated to demystifying Threat Modeling and illuminating its pivotal role in the development of robust security strategies. By starting with Threat Modeling before delving into other technical topics, we aim to establish a framework that informs and enhances all subsequent security efforts.

Threat Modeling is the process of identifying, assessing, and prioritizing potential threats to system security. It serves as a proactive approach, enabling security teams to anticipate vulnerabilities, evaluate potential impacts, and implement effective countermeasures before an attack occurs. This methodical analysis is not just a preliminary step but a continuous practice that guides the secure development lifecycle, from design to deployment and beyond.

Threat Modeling holds paramount importance in cybersecurity architecture for the following reasons:

Proactive Defense: In a landscape where attackers constantly evolve their tactics, a reactive security posture is no longer sufficient. Threat Modeling empowers organizations to adopt a proactive stance, identifying and mitigating risks before they can be exploited.

Strategic Focus: By understanding the most significant threats specific to their environment, organizations can allocate resources more effectively, focusing on the areas of highest risk and potential impact.

Enhanced Security Posture: Through regular and systematic threat analysis, organizations can enhance their overall security posture, making their networks and systems more resilient to attacks.

Informed Decision-Making: Threat Modeling provides critical insights that inform decision-making processes, from selecting security technologies to developing policies and procedures that protect against identified threats.

Compliance and Trust: In an era where regulatory requirements are stringent and customer trust is paramount, demonstrating a commitment to security through Threat Modeling can help meet compliance obligations and build trust with stakeholders.

Starting with Threat Modeling allows us to frame subsequent discussions on cybersecurity within a context of understanding and preparedness. It ensures that as we explore more technical topics, such as encryption, network security, and incident response, our strategies are grounded in a comprehensive understanding of the threats we aim to thwart. This approach not only enhances the effectiveness of technical defenses but also fosters a culture of security that permeates every aspect of the organization.

As we proceed, keep in mind that Threat Modeling is not a one-time task but a dynamic process that evolves with our digital environments. It is the lens through which we can view the cybersecurity landscape, enabling us to navigate it more safely and confidently. Welcome to the critical first step in building a secure foundation for the digital age.

Why security requirements are hard

From the paper "Software Security Assurance State-of-art Report", there are a few findings on why it is hard to get security requirements.

1. The people involved are not likely to know or care (in a conscious sense) about non-functional requirements. Stakeholders have a tendency to take for granted non-functional security needs.

2. Traditional techniques and guidelines tend to be more focused on functional requirements.

3. Security controls are perceived to limit functionality or interfere with usability.

4. It is more difficult to specify what a system should not do than what it should do.

5. Stakeholders must understand the threats facing a system in order to build defense against them, but the threat environment faced by the delivered system will be different from the threat environment existing at the time of requirements development because the threats are evolving.

6. The users who help define the system are not typically the abusers from whom the system must be protected.

Goertzel, K. M., Winograd, T., McKinley, H. L., Oh, L., Colon, M., McGibbon, T.,... Vienneau, R. (2007). Software Security Assurance State-of-art Report (SOAR). Information Assurance Technology Analysis Center (IATAC); Data and Analysis Center for Software (DACS). Herdon, VA: Information Assurance Technology Analysis Center (IATAC).

When you delve deeper into this topic on the difficulty in gathering security requirements, it becomes evident through the lens of threat modeling. Security requirements are challenging for several reasons:

Complexity of Systems: Modern systems are complex, often comprising multiple components that interact in dynamic and sometimes unexpected ways. This complexity makes it difficult to identify all potential security vulnerabilities and to ensure that security measures are comprehensive.

Evolving Threat Landscape: The nature of cyber threats is continuously changing, with attackers constantly devising new techniques and strategies. This evolution means that security requirements must be adaptable and forward-thinking, anticipating future threats rather than merely responding to the current ones.

Balancing Act: Crafting security requirements involves balancing security with usability, performance, and cost. Overly stringent security measures may impair user experience or prove prohibitively expensive, while too lax security can leave systems vulnerable to attack.

Human Factors: Security is not solely a technical challenge but also a human one. Users may inadvertently compromise security through simple errors or misunderstandings, making it essential that security requirements are not only technically sound but also understandable and actionable by all stakeholders.

Regulatory and Compliance Requirements: Navigating the complex landscape of legal, regulatory, and compliance requirements adds another layer of difficulty. Organizations must ensure that their security measures not only protect against threats but also comply with relevant laws and standards.

What are the various threat modeling views

As described earlier, threat modeling is a structured approach that enables organizations to identify, quantify, and address the security threats to a system. It serves as a proactive measure to ensure system security by identifying potential threats and vulnerabilities early in the design process, thereby allowing for the implementation of appropriate security measures to mitigate risk. This methodology is integral to developing a robust security strategy, as it shifts the focus from reacting to incidents to preventing them before they occur. At its core, threat modeling involves a series of steps:

Identifying Security Objectives: Clearly defining what needs to be protected (e.g., data, assets, systems) and understanding the security requirements.

Creating an Architecture Overview: Diagramming and documenting the system architecture, including data flow, to understand how components interact and where sensitive data resides.

Decomposing the System or Application: Breaking down the system or application into its components, processes, and data flows to identify potential security vulnerabilities.

Identifying Threats: Using various methodologies to enumerate potential threats to each component of the system.

Documenting and Prioritizing Threats: Assessing the severity and potential impact of each threat to prioritize mitigation efforts.

Defining and Implementing Mitigations: Developing strategies to mitigate or eliminate identified threats, and integrating these strategies into the project lifecycle.

Various Models of Threat Modeling

Several methodologies and frameworks have been developed to guide the threat modeling process, each with its own focus and techniques. Some of the most widely used models include:

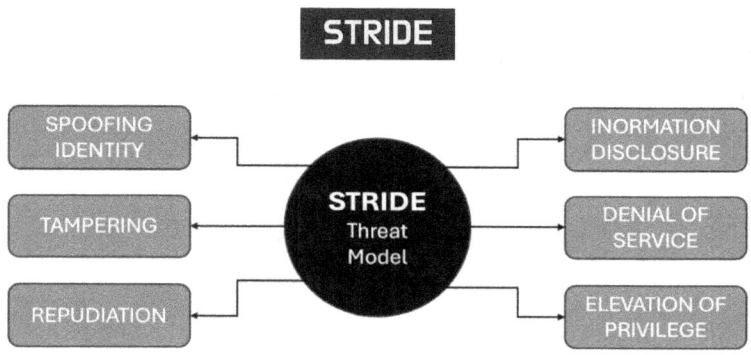

Developed by Microsoft, STRIDE is an acronym for Spoofing, Tampering, Repudiation, Information Disclosure, Denial of Service, and Elevation of Privilege. This model helps in identifying threats by categorizing them into one of these six classes.STRIDE is one of the most widely used threat modeling methodologies. It provides a mnemonic for remembering the six categories of security threats it covers:

Spoofing: An attacker impersonating something or someone else to gain unauthorized access to systems or information. This can involve the falsification of emails, IP addresses, or other identifying information.

Tampering: The unauthorized modification of data or system functions. Tampering can occur in transit or within the system itself, altering logs, data files, or even executable binaries to perform malicious actions or hide activities.

Repudiation: The ability of an attacker to deny having performed an action, typically due to the lack of sufficient logging, monitoring, and auditing controls. This makes it difficult to prove wrongdoing or trace actions back to their source.

Information Disclosure: Unauthorized access to or exposure of confidential information, which could include personal data, trade secrets, or sensitive corporate information. This can result from flaws in software, misconfigurations, or inadequate access controls.

Denial of Service (DoS): Any attack that aims to make a resource (such as a website, application, or service) unavailable to its intended users. This can be achieved through overwhelming the resource with traffic or exploiting vulnerabilities that cause it to crash.

Elevation of Privilege: An attacker gaining higher access levels than initially granted, often by exploiting vulnerabilities in software or configuration mistakes. This allows attackers to perform unauthorized actions, such as accessing sensitive data, modifying system configurations, or creating additional accounts with elevated rights.

By systematically considering each of these threat categories during the design and development of a system, organizations can identify potential vulnerabilities early and implement appropriate countermeasures to mitigate risks.

As the STRIDE model does not rank the threats, it is often used with DREAD to evaluate and prioritize the potential risks associated with software and system vulnerabilities. It's an acronym that stands for Damage, Reproducibility, Exploitability, Affected users, and Discoverability. Each of these categories is used to score a particular vulnerability or threat, usually on a scale from 0 to 10, allowing organizations to assess the severity and prioritize their response accordingly. Here's a breakdown of each component:

Damage Potential: This measures the potential damage if the vulnerability is exploited. This could range from minimal impact, like a small breach of non-sensitive data, to severe impact, such as complete system takeover or exposure of sensitive data.

Reproducibility: This assesses how easy it is to reproduce the attack. If an attack can be easily repeated by an attacker without specialized knowledge, tools, or conditions, it scores higher in this category.

Exploitability: This considers how easy it is to exploit the vulnerability. It takes into account the level of access or privileges required, the complexity of the attack, and whether an attack can be executed remotely or requires physical access.

Affected Users: This evaluates the proportion of users or systems that would be impacted by an exploit. A vulnerability that affects a larger number of users or critical systems scores higher.

Discoverability: This measures how easy it is for potential attackers to discover the vulnerability. A flaw that is easy to find or well-documented in public sources scores higher in this category.

Organizations use DREAD as part of their security risk assessment processes to quantify, compare, and prioritize risks. By evaluating each threat against these five criteria, teams can better understand the potential impact of vulnerabilities and allocate resources more effectively to mitigate the most significant risks.

However, it's worth noting that while DREAD provides a structured approach to evaluating threats, its effectiveness can vary depending on how consistently the scoring criteria are applied. It's also been criticized for its subjective nature, as different evaluators might score the same vulnerability differently. Therefore, some organizations modify the DREAD model or use it in conjunction with other risk assessment methods to suit their specific needs and objectives.

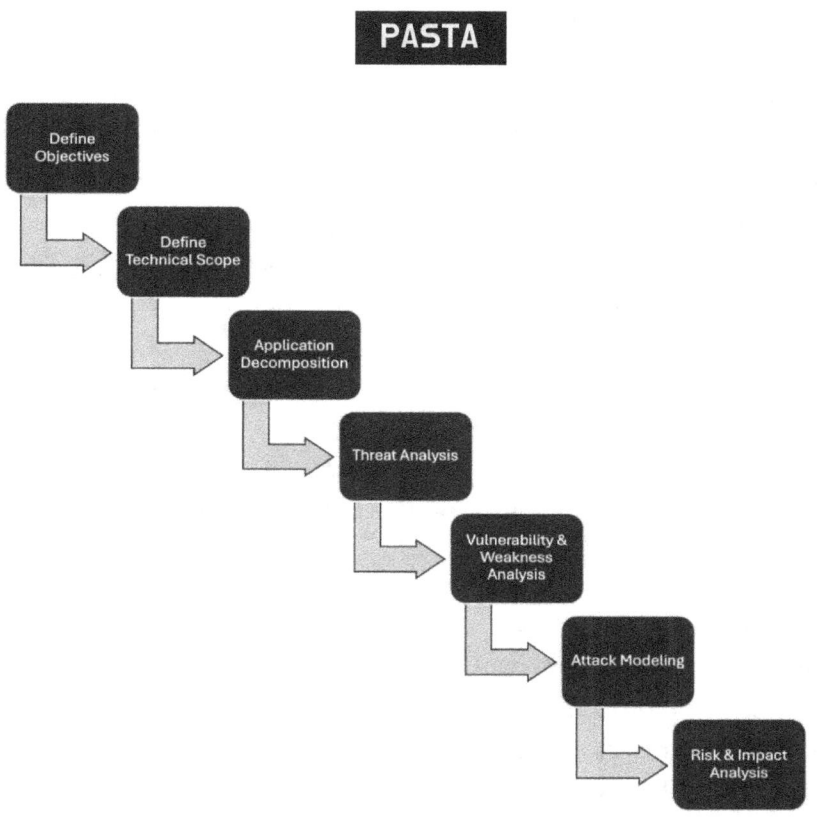

PASTA, which stands for **Process for Attack Simulation and Threat Analysis**, is a comprehensive, risk-centric threat modeling framework. It was designed to integrate security and risk management into the development process, offering a detailed, seven-step methodology that guides organizations through the process of identifying, assessing, and mitigating threats in a structured and thorough manner. PASTA is particularly notable for its emphasis on aligning technical threats with business objectives and risks, making it a valuable tool for ensuring that security measures are directly relevant to the protection of critical business assets.

The Seven Steps of PASTA

Define Objectives: The first step involves understanding and defining the business objectives and technical scope of the system or application. This includes identifying critical assets, functionalities, and the overall purpose of the system from a business perspective. This step ensures that the threat modeling process remains aligned with the business's needs and priorities.

Define Technical Scope: This involves detailed documentation of the system architecture, including data flows, inputs, outputs, and components. Understanding the technical scope is crucial for identifying where valuable assets are located, how they are processed, and through what channels they are communicated.

Application Decomposition: In this phase, the system is broken down into its smallest components, such as processes, data stores, and communication paths. This granular view helps in identifying potential security weaknesses and the various ways in which an attacker could interact with the system.

Threat Analysis: This step involves identifying potential threats to the system using a structured approach, such as STRIDE, to categorize different types of threats. The aim is to systematically consider all possible vectors of attack that could be exploited by adversaries.

Vulnerability and Weakness Analysis: Building on the identified threats, this phase focuses on pinpointing specific vulnerabilities and weaknesses within the system that could be exploited by those threats. This analysis often involves both automated tools and manual review to assess the system against known vulnerabilities and security best practices.

Attack Modeling: Here, potential attacks are modeled based on the identified threats and vulnerabilities. This involves simulating attack paths and scenarios to understand how an attacker might exploit vulnerabilities to compromise the system. This step is crucial for prioritizing which vulnerabilities to address based on their exploitability and potential impact.

Risk and Impact Analysis: The final step involves assessing the identified threats and vulnerabilities in terms of their potential impact on the business and the likelihood of their exploitation. This risk analysis helps prioritize security efforts based on the severity and likelihood of each threat, ensuring that resources are allocated effectively to mitigate the most significant risks.

Key Features of PASTA

Risk-Centric: PASTA focuses on aligning security efforts with business risks, ensuring that security measures are directly relevant to protecting critical business assets and objectives.

Comprehensive: By covering everything from business objectives to attack simulation, PASTA provides a thorough framework for identifying and mitigating threats.

Flexible: While PASTA is a structured approach, it is also flexible enough to be adapted to different types of applications and business environments.

Iterative: PASTA encourages an iterative approach to threat modeling, where the process is repeated as new information becomes available or as the system evolves.

PASTA's comprehensive and risk-centric approach makes it particularly effective for organizations that seek to integrate security considerations deeply within their development processes, ensuring that security measures are both effective and aligned with business priorities.

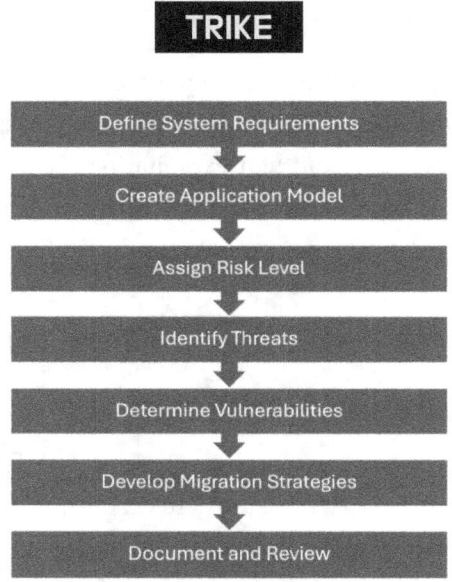

TRIKE is a risk management-oriented framework that starts by defining a security model for the system and uses this model to derive security requirements and evaluate the system's risk posture. Trike revolves around a few key components that differentiate it from other threat modeling approaches:

Risk Framework: At its core, Trike is built around a rigorous risk framework that categorizes security concerns in terms of risks to the system. It uses this framework to systematically identify and assess threats, vulnerabilities, and the potential impact of security breaches on the organization's objectives.

Data-centric Analysis: Trike places a strong emphasis on data - how it is stored, processed, and transmitted within the system. By focusing on data, Trike seeks to identify what needs to be protected most and how data can be compromised, ensuring that security measures are data-centric.

Actor and Action Modeling: Trike models the system from the perspective of different actors (both legitimate users and potential attackers) and their possible actions. This approach helps in understanding how different actors interact with the system and how unauthorized actions could lead to security breaches.

The Trike Methodology Process

The Trike methodology process can be broken down into several stages, each designed to systematically address different aspects of the threat modeling:

Define Security Requirements: The first step involves defining clear, actionable security requirements based on the organization's risk tolerance and the value of the assets being protected. These requirements should be specific, measurable, and tied directly to the organization's objectives.

Create Application Model: This involves creating a detailed model of the application or system, including its components, data flows, and interactions. This model serves as the basis for identifying potential threats and vulnerabilities.

Assign Risk Levels: Based on the application model, risk levels are assigned to different components and data flows, reflecting the potential impact of a security breach. This step helps prioritize security efforts according to the risk associated with different parts of the system.

Identify Threats: Using the application model and risk levels, Trike then identifies potential threats to the system. This includes both external threats from attackers and internal threats, such as system failures or misuse by legitimate users.

Determine Vulnerabilities: Once threats have been identified, the next step is to determine specific vulnerabilities that could be exploited by those threats. This involves a detailed analysis of the system's design, implementation, and configuration.

Develop Mitigation Strategies: For each identified vulnerability, Trike recommends developing specific mitigation strategies. These strategies could involve technical fixes, changes in processes, or enhancements to monitoring and response capabilities.

Document and Review: The final step involves documenting the threat model, including the identified threats, vulnerabilities, and mitigation strategies, and reviewing it with stakeholders. This documentation serves as a living document that can be updated as the system evolves or as new threats emerge.

Key Features of Trike

Risk-Based Approach: Trike's focus on risk management ensures that security measures are aligned with the organization's overall risk posture and business objectives.

Stakeholder Engagement: By producing understandable and actionable security models, Trike encourages engagement and collaboration among all stakeholders, ensuring that security is integrated throughout the organization.

Adaptability: Trike is designed to be adaptable to different types of systems and organizations, allowing for customization based on specific security needs and risk tolerance levels.

In summary, Trike offers a comprehensive and risk-based approach to threat modeling, emphasizing the importance of data protection, stakeholder engagement, and alignment with business objectives. Its structured process helps organizations identify, assess, and mitigate security threats in a way that is both strategic and actionable.

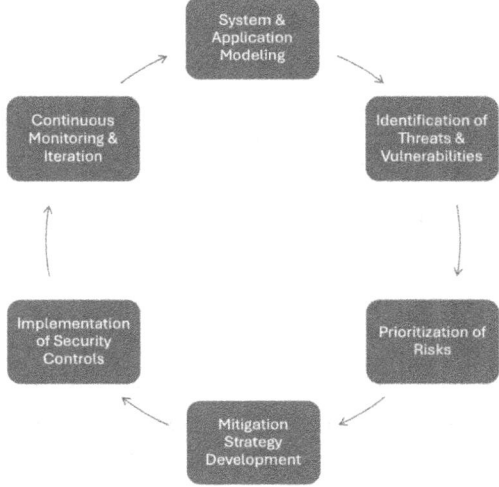

VAST advocates for a scalable, enterprise-wide approach to threat modeling, aiming to be both visually understandable and agile enough to be integrated into continuous development processes. The Visual, Agile, and Simple Threat (VAST) model is a threat modeling approach designed to address some of the challenges associated with traditional threat modeling methodologies in large, complex, and agile environments. VAST distinguishes itself by promoting a more holistic, scalable, and collaborative approach, making it particularly suitable for organizations that employ agile development practices or have large-scale, distributed systems.

Core Principles of VAST

The VAST model is built around several core principles that help it stand out from other threat modeling approaches:

Visual: VAST emphasizes the use of visual representations to map out the system architecture, data flows, and potential threats. These visual diagrams make it easier for diverse stakeholders, including those who are not security experts, to understand the system's security posture and participate in the threat modeling process.

Agile: Recognizing the dynamic nature of agile development environments, VAST is designed to be flexible and iterative. It can be seamlessly integrated into continuous integration/continuous deployment (CI/CD) pipelines, ensuring that threat modeling is an ongoing process that evolves alongside the system.

Simple: VAST aims to simplify the threat modeling process, making it accessible to all members of a project team, not just security specialists. This simplicity encourages broader participation in the security design and decision-making process.

The VAST Methodology Process

The VAST methodology process involves several key steps designed to integrate seamlessly with agile development practices:

System and Application Modeling: Initially, the system or application is modeled using visual diagrams that capture its architecture, components, and data flows. This modeling is not a one-time effort but an iterative process that updates the diagrams as the system evolves.

Identification of Threats and Vulnerabilities: With the system modeled visually, teams identify potential threats and vulnerabilities that could impact the system. This identification leverages both automated tools and manual analysis to ensure comprehensive coverage.

Prioritization of Risks: Risks are then prioritized based on factors such as potential impact and likelihood of occurrence. This prioritization helps focus attention and resources on the most significant threats.

Mitigation Strategy Development: For each high-priority threat, the team develops mitigation strategies. These strategies are designed to be pragmatic and achievable within the agile development cycle.

Implementation of Security Controls: The recommended security controls and mitigation strategies are implemented as part of the regular development sprints. This integration ensures that security considerations are addressed continuously throughout the development process.

Continuous Monitoring and Iteration: Finally, the system is continuously monitored for new threats, and the threat model is updated accordingly. This iterative process ensures that the threat model remains relevant and effective as the system and its threat landscape evolve.

Key Features of VAST

Scalability: VAST is designed to scale with the organization, making it suitable for both small teams and large enterprises.

Integration with Agile and DevOps: By fitting into agile and DevOps workflows, VAST ensures that security is a continuous concern throughout the system's lifecycle.

Collaboration: Encouraging participation from across the organization, VAST helps build a culture of security awareness and shared responsibility.

Flexibility: VAST's flexible approach allows it to adapt to changes in the system or in the threat environment, ensuring that the threat model remains relevant.

In summary, VAST offers an adaptable, scalable, and user-friendly approach to threat modeling, particularly suited to agile environments and organizations with complex, evolving systems. By integrating security considerations into the development process and promoting collaboration across different roles, VAST helps ensure that security is a continuous, shared concern throughout the system's lifecycle.

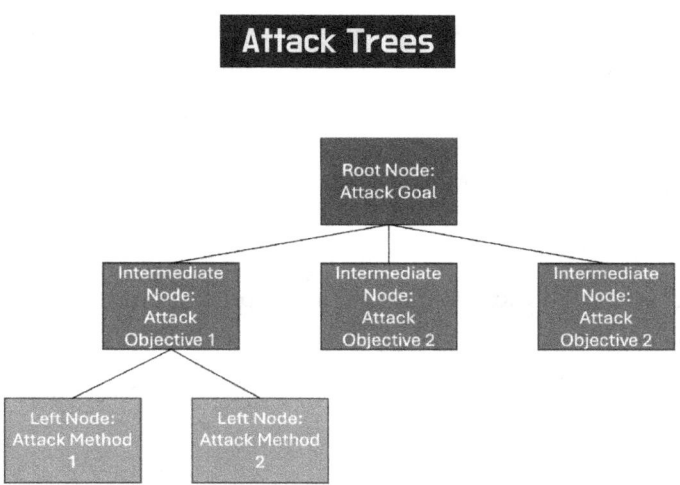

A graphical method of modeling the security of systems based on varying attack scenarios. It helps in visualizing the paths an attacker might take to compromise a system. Attack trees provide a methodical way of describing the security of systems based on varying attack scenarios. They are a graphical representation of how an attacker can potentially compromise a system, breaking down the steps towards achieving a malicious goal into a tree structure. Each node within the tree represents a specific action or choice available to the attacker, with the root node symbolizing the ultimate goal of the attack.

Structure of Attack Trees

Root Node: Represents the primary objective of the attacker, such as stealing sensitive data, disrupting service, or gaining unauthorized access.

Intermediate Nodes: Depict various methods or strategies that can be used to achieve the goal. These are essentially the sub-goals or tactics an attacker might employ.

Leaf Nodes: Represent the specific actions or conditions necessary to achieve the intermediate goals. These are often the most granular actions, such as exploiting a specific vulnerability or bypassing a firewall.

Building and Analyzing Attack Trees

Building an Attack Tree: The process starts with defining the main goal of the attacker and then brainstorming all possible ways that goal could be achieved. These methods are added as branches to the tree, with further details fleshed out in sub-branches as the attack paths are explored more deeply.

Analyzing an Attack Tree: Once constructed, the attack tree can be analyzed to identify the most vulnerable points in the system, determine the complexity of different attack vectors, and evaluate the potential impact of an attack. This analysis often involves:

Prioritizing Threats: Identifying which paths are most likely to be exploited based on factors like the skill level required, resources needed, and potential payoff.

Evaluating Security Measures: Assessing current security measures against the identified attack paths to determine their effectiveness and identify any gaps.

Quantitative Analysis: In some cases, numerical values can be assigned to nodes to estimate probabilities, costs, and impacts, allowing for a more quantitative risk assessment.

Benefits of Attack Trees

Systematic Exploration of Threats: Attack trees help systematically explore and document the various ways a system can be attacked, ensuring a comprehensive understanding of threats.

Visualization: The graphical nature of attack trees makes it easier for security teams, stakeholders, and non-technical personnel to understand the potential attack vectors and security issues.

Prioritization: By breaking down attacks into detailed steps, attack trees help organizations prioritize security measures based on the most likely or damaging attack paths.

Reusable Knowledge: Once created, an attack tree for a specific type of attack or system can be reused or adapted for similar situations, building a knowledge base of security information.

Limitations of Attack Trees

While attack trees are a valuable tool in the threat modeling arsenal, they do have limitations. They can become unwieldy for very complex systems or when considering a wide range of potential attack vectors. Additionally, the effectiveness of attack trees depends on the thoroughness of the analysis and the knowledge of those constructing them. Missing potential attack vectors can lead to gaps in the security strategy.

Attack trees offer a structured and intuitive method for understanding the threats facing a system and planning defenses accordingly. By visualizing the steps an attacker might take to achieve their objectives, attack trees provide valuable insights into security vulnerabilities and help prioritize mitigation efforts effectively. Despite their limitations, when used as part of a comprehensive security analysis and risk management process, attack trees can significantly enhance an organization's ability to defend against potential attacks.

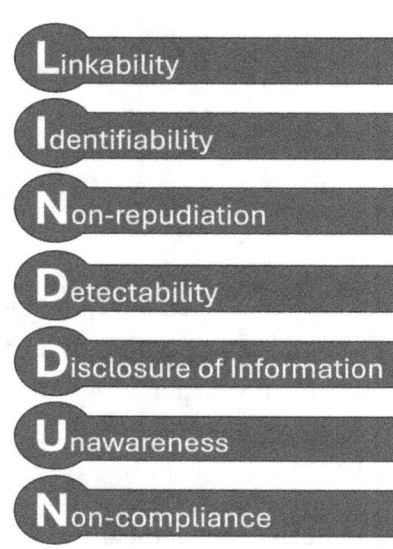

The LINDDUN threat modeling method is a systematic approach designed to identify privacy threats in software systems. It was developed to help software engineers and privacy experts systematically address privacy concerns during the development process. LINDDUN stands for Linkability, Identifiability, Non-repudiation, Detectability, Disclosure of information, Unawareness, and Non-compliance, each representing a different aspect of privacy that could be compromised. Here's a breakdown of each component:

Linkability: This refers to the ability to link at least two items (e.g., messages, actions, subjects, or data) concerning the same user or group of users. Linkability can lead to privacy breaches when an attacker can establish that different pieces of data are related to the same individual.

Identifiability: This is the ability to identify a user or group of users from a set of subjects. A system faces identifiability issues if an attacker can pinpoint a specific user within a group, potentially leading to privacy breaches.

Non-repudiation: Unlike in security contexts where non-repudiation is often desired, in privacy contexts, it can be a threat. This occurs when a user cannot deny the authorship of a message or action, which might be undesirable in situations where anonymity is preferred.

Detectability: This is the ability to discern that an item (e.g., a message, user, or action) exists or an event has occurred. If an attacker can detect sensitive information or actions, it can lead to privacy violations.

Disclosure of information: This threat occurs when confidential or personal information is revealed to unauthorized individuals or entities, compromising the confidentiality of user data.

Unawareness: This refers to a situation where users are unaware of the processing of their personal data. It represents a privacy threat because it denies users the opportunity to consent to or contest the processing and use of their data.

Non-compliance: This threat arises when data processing practices do not comply with legal, regulatory, or contractual obligations concerning privacy. Non-compliance can lead to legal penalties and damage to reputation.

The LINDDUN framework offers a systematic approach to privacy threat modeling through a series of steps that include identifying data flows within a system, applying privacy threat patterns, and determining mitigations for identified threats. It is especially useful for software systems where privacy is a critical concern, providing a structured way to analyze and address potential privacy issues early in the development process.

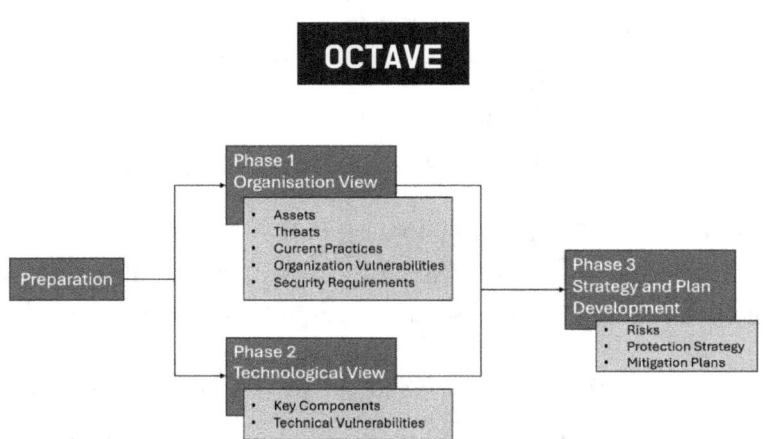

The Operationally Critical Threat, Asset, and Vulnerability Evaluation (OCTAVE) is a comprehensive, self-directed threat modeling approach designed for organizations to assess their information security risks. Developed by the Software Engineering Institute (SEI) at Carnegie Mellon University, OCTAVE emphasizes organizational risk management through a thorough analysis of vulnerabilities, threats, and impacts on critical assets. Unlike other threat modeling methodologies that might focus on technical aspects or specific systems, OCTAVE adopts a broader perspective, integrating organizational, operational, and technological concerns into its risk assessment process.

OCTAVE is characterized by three primary phases: building an organizational view of security, identifying key assets and their vulnerabilities, and developing a security strategy and plans to address identified risks. The initial phase focuses on gathering information to understand the organization's operational context, security requirements, and objectives. This involves engaging with senior management and operational staff to define critical assets—information or systems crucial for the organization's mission.

The second phase dives deeper into the technical and operational environment surrounding these critical assets. Here, the method employs various techniques to identify vulnerabilities in the assets and assesses the threats that could exploit these weaknesses. It involves analyzing current security practices, technologies in use, and potential internal and external threat actors. This phase is particularly participatory, involving workshops and interviews with staff to uncover insights that might not be evident from a purely technical analysis.

In the final phase, OCTAVE guides the organization in developing a practical, strategic approach to mitigate the identified risks. This involves prioritizing risks based on their potential impact on the organization and devising detailed action plans to strengthen security posture. The methodology encourages creating a balanced portfolio of security measures that address both immediate vulnerabilities and longer-term strategic goals.

OCTAVE distinguishes itself by its emphasis on involving a wide range of stakeholders within the organization, recognizing that effective security risk management requires insights from both technical and non-technical personnel. This inclusive approach ensures that the resulting security strategies are aligned with the organization's operational realities and risk tolerance levels.

As a threat modeling methodology, OCTAVE offers organizations a structured way to assess and manage their information security risks comprehensively. By focusing on critical assets and involving stakeholders across the organization, OCTAVE helps in developing informed, strategic responses to the complex landscape of cybersecurity threats.

CVSS (Common Vulnerability Scoring System)

Though not a threat modeling framework per se, CVSS provides a standardized framework for rating the severity of security vulnerabilities, which can be used as part of the threat identification and prioritization process in threat modeling.

The Common Vulnerability Scoring System (CVSS) is a free and open industry standard for assessing the severity of computer system security vulnerabilities. While CVSS itself is not a threat modeling methodology in the traditional sense, it plays a crucial role within the broader context of threat modeling, vulnerability management, and risk assessment. CVSS provides a way to capture the principal characteristics of a vulnerability and produce a numerical score reflecting its severity. This score can then be used to prioritize response and mitigation efforts based on the potential impact of the vulnerability.

Components of CVSS

CVSS scores are calculated using three metric groups that provide a detailed view of the characteristics of a vulnerability:

Base Metrics: These represent the intrinsic qualities of a vulnerability that are constant over time and across user environments. Base metrics include aspects like the complexity of exploiting the vulnerability, the need for user interaction, the impact on confidentiality, integrity, and availability, and more. The base score is a critical component, as it provides a standardized measure of the inherent severity of the vulnerability.

Temporal Metrics: These reflect the characteristics of a vulnerability that may change over time but not across user environments. Temporal metrics include the current exploitability of the vulnerability, the existence of any official fixes, and the confidence in the description and details of the vulnerability. The temporal score can adjust the base score up or down based on these factors.

Environmental Metrics: Environmental metrics allow the score to be customized based on the importance of the affected IT asset to a user's organization, the presence of mitigations, and how the vulnerability impacts this specific environment. This customization is crucial for organizations to prioritize vulnerabilities based on their unique context.

How CVSS Supports Threat Modeling

In the context of threat modeling, CVSS serves as a tool for prioritizing vulnerabilities that have been identified during the threat analysis phase. By providing a standardized way to rate the severity of vulnerabilities, CVSS helps organizations focus their efforts on the most critical issues that could be exploited by threats. Here's how CVSS complements threat modeling:

Prioritization: CVSS scores help organizations prioritize vulnerabilities based on their severity, ensuring that resources are allocated to mitigate the most significant risks first.

Risk Assessment: By integrating CVSS scores into their broader risk assessment processes, organizations can better understand the potential impact of vulnerabilities within the context of their specific environment.

Communication: CVSS provides a common language for describing the severity of vulnerabilities across different stakeholders, facilitating clearer communication about security risks.

Limitations of CVSS

While CVSS is a powerful tool for vulnerability management, it's important to note that it does not encompass all aspects of threat modeling. CVSS scores focus on the severity of vulnerabilities rather than the broader context of threats, such as the capabilities or intentions of attackers. Therefore, CVSS should be used as part of a comprehensive threat modeling and risk management process that also considers the likelihood of a vulnerability being exploited and the potential impact on the organization.

In summary, CVSS is an essential component of the vulnerability management and risk assessment processes, providing a standardized way to assess the severity of security vulnerabilities. When used in conjunction with threat modeling methodologies, CVSS helps organizations prioritize security efforts effectively, ensuring that they can respond to the most critical threats in a timely and informed manner.

MITRE ATT&CK Framework

MITRE ATT&CK

Like CVSS above, the MITRE ATT&CK framework is not in itself a that modeling method. The MITRE ATT&CK framework is a comprehensive matrix of tactics and techniques that describe various cyber adversary behaviors based on real-world observations. ATT&CK stands for Adversarial Tactics, Techniques, and Common Knowledge. The framework is developed and maintained by MITRE, a not-for-profit organization that operates research and development centers sponsored by the federal government of the United States. It is widely used by cybersecurity professionals to understand threat actor behaviors, develop effective defense strategies, and improve the overall security posture of organizations.

Components of MITRE ATT&CK

The framework is organized into matrices that cover different operational environments, such as Enterprise, Mobile, and Cloud. Each matrix consists of:

Tactics: These represent the "why" of an ATT&CK technique, describing the adversary's goals or objectives (e.g., Initial Access, Execution, Persistence). Tactics provide context to the techniques and help understand the purpose behind them.

Techniques: These detail "how" an adversary achieves a tactical goal by describing the action taken (e.g., Spear Phishing, Exploit Public-Facing Application). Techniques are the specific methods used to accomplish a tactic.

Sub-techniques: These provide a more detailed breakdown of techniques, offering granularity on the specific ways an adversary can perform a technique.

Mitigations: These are recommendations for preventing or limiting the effectiveness of techniques.

Detection: This outlines ways to identify the technique being used, helping defenders spot adversary activities.

Using MITRE ATT&CK for Threat Modeling

Similar to CVSS, the MITRE ATT&CK framework aids in this process of threat modeling by providing a structured way to identify and understand the tactics and techniques that adversaries might use against an organization's systems. Here's how it is applied in threat modeling:

Identify Relevant Tactics and Techniques: Organizations can use the ATT&CK framework to identify which tactics and techniques are relevant to their specific context, based on their industry, size, geography, or specific threat intelligence.

Map Threat Actor Profiles: By understanding the behaviors of specific threat actors or groups, organizations can map these to the ATT&CK framework to anticipate potential attacks and prioritize defenses accordingly.

Assessment and Gap Analysis: The framework allows organizations to assess their current security controls against the techniques listed in ATT&CK to identify gaps in their defenses.

Inform Defense Strategies: Using insights from the framework, organizations can develop or enhance their defensive strategies to address identified tactics and techniques, focusing on detection, mitigation, and prevention.

Continuous Improvement: As the ATT&CK framework is regularly updated with new tactics, techniques, and mitigation advice, organizations can continually refine their security posture in response to evolving threats.

The MITRE ATT&CK framework is a valuable resource for threat modeling, offering a detailed and actionable catalog of adversary behaviors and techniques. By integrating the framework into their threat modeling processes, organizations can enhance their ability to identify, understand, and mitigate cyber threats effectively.

Each of these models brings a unique perspective to threat modeling, allowing organizations to choose or adapt the framework that best fits their specific needs and the nature of their systems. By applying these models, organizations can systematically understand and mitigate the risks their systems face, thus enhancing their overall security posture. Threat modeling is an approach for analyzing the security of an application. It is a structured approach that enables you to identify, quantify, and address the security risks associated with an application.

Persona non Grata

The "Persona non Grata" threat model refers to a category of threat where the malicious actor is identified as an unwelcome or undesired individual within the context of the system being protected. This can be an insider threat or a previously identified external threat. The term "Persona non Grata" is a Latin expression that means "an unwelcome person" and has been adapted in cybersecurity to identify and describe threats posed by individuals who are to be excluded from access to the system due to their intent to harm.

The focus of the Persona non Grata model is to identify, profile, and understand the potential attacker who has motivations to target the system. This model is less about technical vulnerabilities and more about understanding human behavior and motivations. It involves creating detailed profiles for potential attackers, which include their skills, resources, motivations, and potential methods of attack. Here's how this can be applied:

Identifying Potential Personas: Organizations identify different types of attackers that may want to harm the system. This can include disgruntled employees, ex-employees with grudges, business competitors, activists, or state-sponsored agents.

Motivation and Goals: Understanding what drives these attackers helps predict potential targets and methods. For example, a disgruntled employee may seek to damage the company's reputation, steal intellectual property, or disrupt operations.

Access and Skills: Determining the level of access (physical or logical) and technical skills the persona has informs what they might be capable of doing. An insider with access to sensitive areas may exploit their position, while an outsider might require more sophisticated methods to gain access.

Mitigation Strategies: Strategies can be developed to address the specific threats posed by these personas. For disgruntled employees, this might involve better access controls, monitoring, and segregation of duties. For external threats, more robust perimeter defenses and anomaly detection might be prioritized.

The Persona non Grata threat model is particularly useful for tailoring security measures to the most dangerous and likely threats an organization faces. By anticipating the actions of potential attackers, security teams can prepare more effective defenses and response plans.

Threat Modeling Views

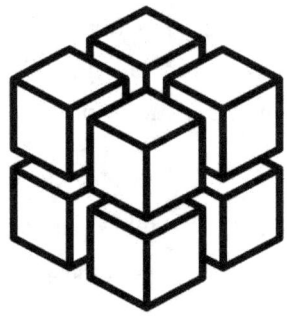

As threat modeling is a process used to proactively identify, assess, and address potential security threats to a system, it involves understanding the system from various perspectives to better identify where threats could arise and how they could be mitigated. These perspectives include the functional view, deployment view, data flow view, environmental view, and social view. Each provides a unique lens through which the system can be analyzed for vulnerabilities:

Functional View

This perspective focuses on the functionality and structure of the system without considering its physical realization. It looks at the components of the system, such as software modules, libraries, and the interactions between them. The functional view in threat modeling focuses on the system's functionalities and how they are achieved, analyzing the system through the lens of its features and behaviors. This perspective is particularly useful for identifying threats that could exploit the specific ways in which a system's functions are implemented and interact. It involves breaking down the system into its constituent functions and examining the potential security vulnerabilities within those functions.

Examples of the Functional View in Threat Modeling

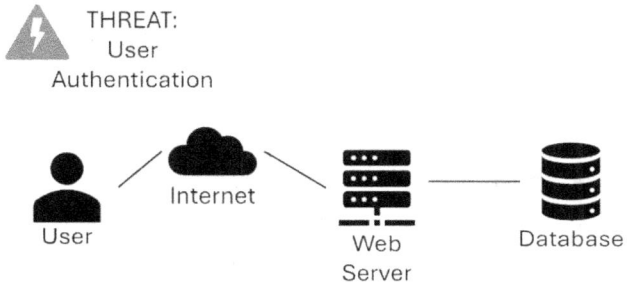

Web Application: Consider a web application that includes user authentication, form submission for data entry, and a payment gateway for transactions. The functional view would dissect these features to identify vulnerabilities such as:

User Authentication: Threats could include brute force attacks, password cracking, and session hijacking. The functional view would help in identifying weak authentication mechanisms.

Form Submission: This functionality could be susceptible to SQL injection attacks, cross-site scripting (XSS), and other forms of data validation vulnerabilities that could allow attackers to inject malicious code or extract sensitive data.

Payment Gateway: Threats could involve interception of payment information, manipulation of transaction data, or replay attacks. The functional view would highlight the need for secure communication protocols, input validation, and other security measures.

Internet of Things (IoT) Device: An IoT device that monitors environmental conditions and sends data to a central server could be examined for:

> **Data Transmission**: Potential vulnerabilities might include the interception of data in transit, necessitating the examination of encryption protocols and data integrity checks.
>
> **Device Authentication**: The process of the device authenticating to the network or server could be threatened by impersonation attacks, pointing to the need for robust device identity management.
>
> **Sensor Data Processing**: The handling of data from sensors might be vulnerable to spoofing or injection attacks, indicating the importance of validating and sanitizing sensor inputs.

Mobile Application: A mobile app that offers location-based services, social networking, and private messaging might be analyzed for:

> **Location Services**: Threats could involve unauthorized access to location data, necessitating strict access controls and user consent mechanisms.
>
> **Social Networking Features**: Vulnerabilities might include privacy breaches through profile enumeration or manipulation, highlighting the need for secure data handling and privacy settings.
>
> **Private Messaging**: Potential threats could involve eavesdropping on messages or data leakage, underscoring the importance of end-to-end encryption and secure data storage.

The functional view is crucial for understanding how a system's specific features and behaviors could be targeted by threats. By focusing on the functionalities, threat modelers can identify security requirements and design countermeasures that address the vulnerabilities inherent in how the system operates. This ensures that security measures are not just applied broadly but are tailored to protect the system's particular functions and the data they handle or generate.

Deployment View

The deployment view examines how the system is distributed across physical and virtual resources. It considers servers, networks, devices, and their configurations. This perspective helps identify vulnerabilities related to the specific technologies used, network topology, and the security of communication between components. Threats such as network eavesdropping, man-in-the-middle attacks, and system exploitation due to misconfigurations are typically assessed through this view. The deployment view is akin to surveying the battlefield before an engagement. It is the art of discerning the positioning of one's forces and fortifications, assessing the lay of the land to anticipate potential attack vectors.

As we initiate our exploration, we first delineate the territory – the network topology, the distribution of servers across on-premises and cloud environments, the workstations dotting the landscape of an office floor, or the myriad IoT devices embedded across a smart infrastructure. Each element, each node on this map, represents a potential foothold for adversaries.

The threats that emerge within this view are as diverse as the landscape itself. They range from the physical – such as the risk of unauthorized access to server rooms – to the digital – like the exposure of sensitive data through misconfigured cloud storage permissions. The interconnected nature of these components means that a breach in one can cascade, undermining the fortress from within.

Take, for instance, a scenario where a company's servers are deployed both within an on-premises data center and across multiple cloud service providers. The deployment view would consider the security implications of this hybrid setup. It would question how security policies are synchronized between the environments and how data is protected as it travels the network corridors between cloud and physical servers.

Here are 4 examples of threats you can model from a deployment view perspective:

Example 1: Cloud-Based Web Application

A web application deployed in a cloud environment might use a variety of services such as virtual machines, databases, and storage buckets across multiple regions.

Threats	Mitigation
Unauthorized access to cloud management console	Enforce multi-factor authentication and strict access controls for the cloud management console
Misconfiguration of security groups or network access control lists (ACLs)	Regularly audit security group and ACL configurations
Data breaches due to improperly secured storage buckets	Implement encryption and access policies for storage buckets

Example 2: Corporate Network

A corporate network might include workstations, internal servers, and network devices such as routers and firewalls.

Threats	Mitigation
Internal network intrusion due to weak firewall rules	Employ a default-deny firewall policy and rigorously define exceptions
Lateral movement within the network after initial compromise	Segment the network and use intrusion detection/prevention systems (IDS/IPS)
Data exfiltration through unmonitored network exit points	Monitor outbound traffic for anomalies and unauthorized data transfers

Example 3: Internet of Things (IoT) Deployment

IoT devices are often deployed in various physical locations and connect back to central servers or cloud platforms.

Threats	Mitigation
Physical tampering with exposed IoT devices	Use tamper-evident hardware and secure boot mechanisms
Interception of data transmitted over the network	Encrypt data in transit and validate device firmware
Compromise of the central server leading to a takeover of IoT devices	Harden the security of the central server and implement device authentication

Example 4: Hybrid IT Environment

A hybrid IT environment that combines on-premises data centers with cloud services.

Threats	Mitigation
Inconsistent security policies across environments	Harmonize security policies for both on-premises and cloud components
Unsecured data transfer between on-premises and cloud	Use encrypted connections (VPN, TLS) for data in transit
Compromised cloud environment affecting on-premises systems	Implement strong isolation mechanisms between cloud and on-premises systems

In each of these examples, the deployment view helps to identify the unique threats that arise from how and where the system components are deployed. It allows security professionals to tailor their defenses to the specific characteristics of the system's deployment, taking into account the physical and logical connections, the trust boundaries, and the specific technologies and platforms used.

Data Flow View

The data flow view in threat modeling is a perspective that focuses on tracing how data moves through a system. This perspective focuses on the movement of data throughout the system, mapping out how data is input, processed, stored, and output. By examining the paths that data takes, this view helps identify potential points of interception, manipulation, or unauthorized access. Understanding the data flow is crucial for identifying potential vulnerabilities and the points where data could be at risk. This perspective involves creating data flow diagrams (DFDs) that visually represent the flow of data and help in pinpointing where protective measures should be applied.

Let's consider an e-commerce website where users can browse items, add them to a shopping cart, and proceed to checkout by entering personal and payment information.

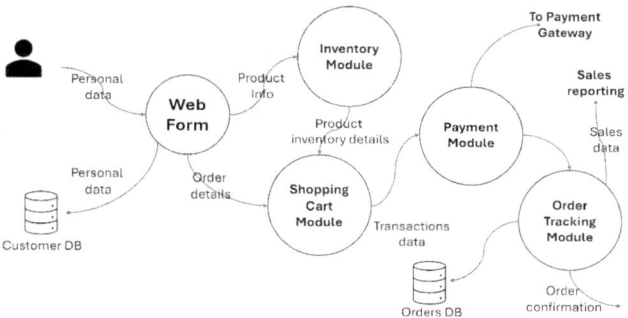

In this case, the **Data Entry Point** could be users entering personal data such as names, addresses, and credit card information via web forms.

The **Data Processing Steps** would include the website server processes the data, checking inventory levels and calculating total costs; and also when payment processing occurs, involving communication with a payment gateway to authorize transactions.

Data Storage Location would be a customer database where the data is stored and also all transaction data is logged for order fulfillment and future customer service needs.

Data Exit Points could be order confirmations and shipping notifications that are sent to the user via email; and aggregated sales data that might be sent to external analytics services for market analysis.

Threats	Mitigation
Interception: Data could be intercepted during transmission if not properly encrypted, for example, through a man-in-the-middle attack.	Use HTTPS to secure data in transit.
Unauthorized Access: Databases containing personal and payment information could be accessed by unauthorized users if database permissions are not correctly set.	Employ proper access controls and authentication for database access.
Injection Attacks: The web form could be vulnerable to SQL injection if the input is not correctly sanitized, potentially allowing attackers to manipulate the database.	Validate and sanitize all inputs to protect against injection attacks. Regularly update and patch all systems to protect against known vulnerabilities.

In creating the data flow diagrams and conducting the analysis, several key components are considered:

Actors: Any entity (user, system, etc.) that provides or can access the data.

Processes: Functions or services that manipulate the data.

Data Stores: Repositories where data resides for any amount of time.

Data Flows: The channels through which data travels from one part of the system to another.

By mapping these components and their interactions, the data flow view helps in identifying where sensitive data might be exposed to threats. This understanding enables security professionals to design and implement controls that are tailored to protect the data effectively as it moves through the system, thereby reducing the risk of data breaches and ensuring compliance with data protection regulations.

Environmental View

The environmental view in threat modeling considers the wider context in which a system operates, taking into account all external factors that could impact its security. This view broadens the scope beyond the technical architecture to include the physical, social, and political environments that could introduce potential threats. It accounts for the human element, the location of physical assets, third-party integrations, legal and compliance requirements, and even the geopolitical climate that may affect system security. Here are some examples of the various environmental threats.

Physical Environment:

A data center located in a region prone to natural disasters such as earthquakes or floods.

Threats	Mitigation
Damage to the physical infrastructure leading to system downtime or data loss.	Implement disaster recovery plans, maintain off-site backups, and establish redundant systems in geographically diverse locations.

Social Environment:

A mobile application developed for a global audience where different countries have varying sensitivities and regulations regarding content.

Threats	Mitigation
Social engineering attacks tailored to specific cultural contexts; compliance violations due to content restrictions in certain jurisdictions.	Cultural awareness training for staff, regional content filters, and robust user authentication processes.

Regulatory and Compliance Environment:

A healthcare provider using electronic health records (EHR) subject to Health Insurance Portability and Accountability Act (HIPAA) regulations.

Threats	Mitigation
Non-compliance penalties and data breaches resulting from inadequate data protection measures.	Ensure all systems handling EHR are HIPAA compliant, conduct regular audits, and provide staff with privacy training.

Economic Environment:

A start-up operating in a highly competitive market with limited cybersecurity resources.

Threats	Mitigation
Cutting corners on security to reduce costs could lead to vulnerabilities; targeted attacks by competitors.	Prioritize essential security controls, seek third-party security services for cost-effective solutions, and stay informed about competitor activities.

Technological Environment:

An organization still using legacy systems that are no longer supported by the vendor.

Threats	Mitigation
Increased risk of exploitation due to unpatched vulnerabilities; compatibility issues with newer security tools.	Plan and execute a phased upgrade or replacement of legacy systems; employ compensating controls in the interim.

Political and Geopolitical Environment:

A multinational corporation operating in countries with unstable political situations or under economic sanctions.

Threats	Mitigation
Cyber espionage or sabotage as part of political conflict; legal consequences of inadvertently violating sanctions.	Implement strict data handling and access controls, encrypt sensitive communications, and comply with international trade laws.

In each case, the environmental view encourages the consideration of factors outside the immediate technical sphere. It looks at how external forces can impact system security and informs the development of comprehensive security strategies that are well-suited to the specific context in which the system operates. This can lead to more resilient security postures that are capable of withstanding a variety of threats, from the physical to the digital, from the individual to the organizational level.

Social View

This perspective examines the human element of cybersecurity. Different from the social environment view, which looks at the larger social environment, this perspective looks at how users, administrators, and potential attackers interact with the system. The social view helps identify threats related to social engineering, phishing, insider threats, and user error. It emphasizes the importance of security awareness, training, and the design of user interfaces that promote secure behavior.

By examining a system from these diverse perspectives, threat modeling provides a comprehensive approach to identifying potential security issues. It enables teams to prioritize threats based on their likelihood and potential impact, leading to the development of more secure systems. This holistic approach ensures that security considerations are integrated throughout the system's lifecycle, from design through deployment and operation, thereby helping to mitigate risks before they can be exploited by attackers. Threat models can be built from a variety of perspective. Each serves a different need.

The social view of threat modeling focuses on understanding the behaviors, interactions, and dynamics of the people who design, develop, use, and potentially attack the system. Here are some examples of social threat models.

Social Engineering:

A company's employees are targeted by phishing campaigns that mimic internal communications.

Threats	Mitigation
Employees could be tricked into divulging their login credentials or installing malware.	Regular training to recognize phishing attempts, deploying email filters, and implementing two-factor authentication to minimize the damage of compromised credentials.

Insider Threats:

A disgruntled employee with access to sensitive financial systems.

Threats	Mitigation
Malicious actions such as data theft, sabotage, or selling access to confidential information.	Implement the principle of least privilege, conduct regular access reviews, establish behavioral monitoring, and foster a positive work environment.

User Behavior and Awareness:

Users of a social networking platform have a tendency to overshare personal information.

Threats	Mitigation
Information disclosed can be used for identity theft or to craft targeted spear-phishing attacks.	Educate users on the risks of oversharing, provide clear privacy settings, and design the system to encourage secure behavior.

Development and Operations Teams:

Development teams under pressure to meet deadlines might neglect security best practices.

Threats	Mitigation
Introducing vulnerabilities into the system, such as insufficient input validation or incomplete testing.	Integrate security into the development lifecycle (DevSecOps), perform code reviews, and offer incentives for identifying and addressing security issues.

Supply Chain and Third-Party Vendors:

A small vendor in the supply chain with less stringent security controls is responsible for a component of a critical infrastructure system.

Threats	Mitigation
Compromise of the vendor could lead to a breach of the larger system.	Conduct security audits of vendors, establish strict requirements for security practices, and create incident response plans that include third-party components.

Cultural and Organizational Norms:

An organization that values openness may have very permissive access to information and systems.

Threats	Mitigation
Such openness can lead to accidental or intentional misuse of data and systems.	Balance openness with access controls, classify data based on sensitivity, and adopt a security-aware culture that understands the need for protection measures.

The social view emphasizes that while technology can be designed to be secure, it is often the human element that determines the actual level of security. Human behavior is unpredictable, and the complexity of human interactions means that the social view can be one of the most challenging perspectives from which to model threats. Nevertheless, it is also one of the most critical because even the most secure systems can be compromised through social manipulation or insider actions. Understanding and mitigating these risks requires a combination of policy, training, and technology, all aimed at creating a secure and aware organizational culture.

A Threat Modeling Example

Let's consider a real-world example of applying the VAST threat modeling approach to a web-based e-commerce application.

Scope Definition

The scope of the threat modeling exercise is the e-commerce application, including its web front-end, back-end server, database, and external APIs. The goal is to identify potential security threats and vulnerabilities that could compromise customer data, financial transactions, and system integrity.

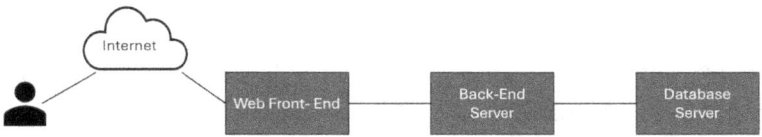

Identify Assets

Assets include customer personal information (e.g., names, addresses, payment details), product catalog, order data, authentication tokens, and the underlying infrastructure (e.g., servers, databases). A data flow diagram visualizes the flow of data between these assets and components. Below are examples of some identified assets.

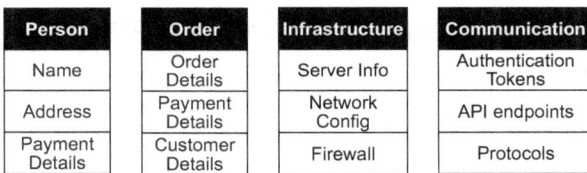

Person	Order	Infrastructure	Communication
Name	Order Details	Server Info	Authentication Tokens
Address	Payment Details	Network Config	API endpoints
Payment Details	Customer Details	Firewall	Protocols

Model Trust Boundaries

Trust boundaries are delineated between the external network (untrusted zone) and the application's internal components (trusted zone). Authentication and authorization mechanisms control access to sensitive functions and data, such as user authentication, session management, and role-based access control.

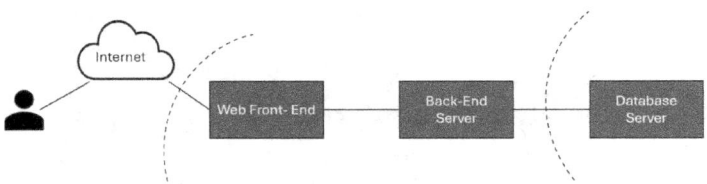

Threat Identification

Using STRIDE, potential threats are identified:

Spoofing: Unauthorized users may attempt to impersonate legitimate customers or administrators.

Tampering: Attackers may manipulate data transmitted between the client and server, such as modifying prices or intercepting payment information.

Repudiation: Users might deny making certain transactions or actions.

Information Disclosure: Sensitive customer data may be exposed through insecure storage, transmission, or inadequate access controls.

Denial of Service: Malicious actors may launch DDoS attacks to disrupt service availability.

Elevation of Privilege: Unauthorized users may exploit vulnerabilities to gain elevated privileges or access unauthorized resources.

Vulnerability Analysis

Vulnerabilities such as SQL injection, cross-site scripting (XSS), insecure direct object references (IDOR), inadequate authentication mechanisms, and insufficient input validation are identified within the application architecture.

Risk Assessment

Risks are assessed based on their severity, likelihood, and potential impact on customer data security, financial transactions, and system availability. High-priority risks include SQL injection leading to data leakage, XSS leading to session hijacking, and inadequate access controls leading to unauthorized data access.

Mitigation Strategies

Mitigation strategies are developed to address identified risks:

1. Implement input validation and parameterized queries to prevent SQL injection.
2. Use secure coding practices and input sanitization to mitigate XSS vulnerabilities.
3. Implement multi-factor authentication and session management best practices to prevent unauthorized access.
4. Encrypt sensitive data at rest and in transit to protect against information disclosure.
5. Implement rate limiting and DDoS protection mechanisms to mitigate denial-of-service attacks.

Documentation and Communication

Findings, risk assessments, and mitigation strategies are documented in a threat model report, accompanied by visual representations, diagrams, and actionable recommendations. The report is communicated to relevant stakeholders, including developers, security teams, and business owners, to raise awareness and prioritize remediation efforts.

Iterative Improvement

The threat model is continuously updated and refined based on ongoing security assessments, penetration testing, and feedback from stakeholders. Changes in the threat landscape, emerging threats, and evolving business requirements are considered to adapt mitigation strategies and improve the overall security posture of the e-commerce application.

By following this example, organizations can effectively apply the VAST threat modeling approach to identify, assess, and mitigate security risks within their e-commerce application architecture, thereby enhancing security, protecting customer data, and maintaining trust in their online business operations.

Enterprise Security Technologies

As organizations expand and diversify, their infrastructures sprawl across a complex web of networks, endpoints, applications, and data stores—each with its own set of vulnerabilities and threats. This myriad of components demands a robust security strategy underpinned by a suite of technologies designed to safeguard the enterprise's most valuable assets. This chapter on "Enterprise Security Technologies" delves into the core areas that are instrumental in fortifying an organization against the multifaceted threats of the modern era. To set the context, below is a diagram to show the various parts of a typical enterprise security deployment.

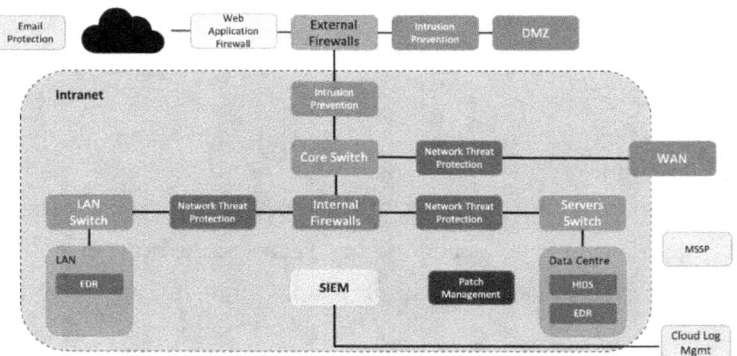

We begin by exploring the intricate world of network security, the bulwark against external and internal threats that traverse the data highways of an organization. As the first line of defense, network security technologies are akin to the fortified walls of a citadel, keeping watch over all incoming and outgoing traffic to thwart unauthorized access and data breaches.

The discourse then transitions to endpoint security, focusing on the devices that serve as the entry points to the enterprise network. In an age where workforces are increasingly mobile, securing these numerous and often remote gateways is akin to outfitting each soldier with the right armor and weapons to defend against any intrusion.

Next, we will examine Identity and Access Management (IAM), a crucial framework that ensures that the right individuals access the appropriate resources at the right times and for the right reasons. Like a vigilant gatekeeper who scrutinizes every entrant, IAM technologies manage users' identities and access privileges with precision and intelligence.

The journey continues with application security, a critical battlefield where much of today's digital skirmishes take place. Here, the code that powers enterprises is dissected, vulnerabilities are hunted down, and defenses are erected to create resilient applications that can withstand the onslaught of attacks.

Data protection, the safeguarding of the lifeblood of the organization—its data—is then explored. This section addresses how modern technologies are employed to encrypt, backup, and secure data both at rest and in transit, effectively creating an impregnable vault for the organization's crown jewels.

Next, we discuss vulnerability and patch management, a fundamental yet often overlooked aspect of IT security. Like maintaining the integrity of a fortress through continuous repairs and upgrades, patch management ensures that vulnerabilities are promptly addressed and systems are kept up to date against the ever-evolving threat landscape.

Lastly, we will cover topics such as supply chain security and mobile devices security, which are areas that are fast growing in any modern organization. Cloud Security as a much larger topic would be covered as a chapter on its own.

This chapter serves as a guide through the landscape of enterprise security technologies. It is a voyage that will equip you with the knowledge to understand, evaluate, and implement the security mechanisms that are vital to the sustenance and success of any modern enterprise. As we navigate each specific area of enterprise security, we will unveil the challenges, solutions, and best practices that form the collective shield guarding organizations against the adversities of the cyber world.

Network Security

In today's hyper-connected world, an enterprise's network is the foundational infrastructure that enables the flow of information and connectivity of services. As the backbone of modern business operations, it is subjected to relentless attempts at unauthorized access, exploitation, and disruption. The section on "Network Security" goes beyond the traditional understanding of network defense—beyond the concept of firewalls as the sole guardians of the network perimeter. Here, we delve into the sophisticated array of technologies and strategies that constitute a robust network security posture for today's enterprises.

Network security in the contemporary context is a multifaceted discipline that encompasses a diverse range of technologies designed to shield the network from a barrage of cyber threats. This section will explore the dynamic nature of Intrusion Detection Systems (IDS) and Intrusion Prevention Systems (IPS), which serve as the vigilant sentinels, constantly monitoring network traffic for signs of malicious activity and taking preemptive actions to thwart potential intrusions.

Further, we will discuss Network Access Control (NAC) solutions that enforce policy-based controls over device access to networks, ensuring that only authenticated and compliant devices can enter and interact with the enterprise's digital resources. As we venture into the realm of network visibility, we will emphasize the criticality of having clear insight into every packet that traverses the network, enabling rapid detection and response to anomalous activity.

However, the domain of network security is not limited to technological solutions alone. Non-technical aspects, particularly regulatory compliance, play a pivotal role in shaping network security strategies.

Adherence to industry standards and legal requirements is not merely about checking boxes but is integral to maintaining trust and operational integrity in a landscape marked by increasing scrutiny and accountability.

This section aims to furnish readers with a comprehensive understanding of modern network security, highlighting that it is a complex blend of technical acumen, strategic foresight, and diligent governance. By recognizing that the defense of an enterprise's network requires more than firewalls—requiring a concerted and multi-layered approach—we prepare you to meet the challenges of securing the critical networks that underpin the digital enterprises of today and tomorrow.

Network Security Tools

For purposes of this book, the network security technologies would be grouped into three categories - Blocking, Inspection, and Monitoring technologies.

Blocking	Inspection	Monitoring
Firewalls	Packet Capture	Network Visibility Tools
IDS/IPS	NetFlow Capture	Log Analysis Tools
Network Access Controls		

Firewalls

Firewalls are a foundational element of network security and act as a barrier between trusted internal networks and untrusted external networks, such as the internet. A firewall can be hardware, software, or a combination of both, and it is used to filter incoming and outgoing network traffic based on an organization's previously established security policies. At its most basic, a firewall can allow or block the flow of traffic.

Firewall technologies has evolved over the years. Here is a quick recap of the evolution of firewalls.

Packet-Filtering Firewalls

The earliest firewalls operated on a simple principle: they would inspect the packets of data attempting to enter the network, checking against rules that assess source and destination IP addresses, port numbers, and the protocol used. While effective at providing a basic level of security, packet-filtering firewalls are limited because they do not inspect the packet contents. They cannot determine if the contents of a packet are malicious.

Stateful Firewalls

Recognizing the need for a more sophisticated approach, stateful firewalls were developed. These inspect the state of active connections and make decisions based on the context of the traffic, not just the individual packets. This type of firewall maintains a table of all ongoing connections and can make more informed blocking decisions by understanding the state of network connections.

Next-Generation Firewalls (NGFW)

Sometime in 2008, Palo Alto Networks introduced the first NGFW. NGFWs introduce deep packet inspection (DPI), which goes beyond basic header information to inspect the data within the packet itself. This allows the firewall to understand the applications that are sending traffic through the network, not just the protocol and ports being used. These new generation of firewalls incorporate extra functionality to improve the security posture of the network. These include:

Intrusion Prevention Systems (IPS)

NGFWs often incorporate intrusion prevention systems, which actively monitor network and/or system activities for malicious activities. The main functions of an intrusion prevention system are to identify malicious activity, log information about this activity, attempt to block/stop it, and report it.

Application Awareness

NGFWs have the ability to understand and filter traffic based on application ID. This means they can control internal and external applications (like Facebook, YouTube, or custom enterprise applications) by allowing or denying traffic on a per-application basis.

Integrated Security Functions

NGFWs integrate a variety of security functions directly into the firewall platform. This can include antivirus, anti-spam, web filtering, and anti-bot features.

Intelligence and Identity

NGFWs can also use external intelligence services to receive updates about current threats, and they can enforce security policies based on user identity, not just IP address, creating rules that adapt to the dynamic nature of user activity.

Advanced Threat Protection

They may include advanced threat protection (ATP) features, such as sandboxing environments, where incoming files are analyzed in a safe, isolated network environment to detect potential zero-day threats.

Integration with Cloud Services

As cloud services become more prevalent, NGFWs are also evolving to provide security in cloud-based environments, protecting traffic not only on-premises but also in the cloud, often through a consistent policy framework.

The progression from basic packet filtering to NGFWs is a response to the continuously evolving security landscape. As threats have become more sophisticated, so too have the tools we use to protect against them. Firewalls have grown from simple network gateways to complex security devices that can adapt to the changing tactics of threat actors, offering deeper inspection and a more integrated approach to network security.

Intrusion Detection/Prevention Systems

Intrusion Detection Systems (IDS) and Intrusion Prevention Systems (IPS) are critical components of network security that help monitor and protect networks from malicious activities and policy violations. While both technologies share a common goal of identifying and dealing with threats, they differ in their approach and functionality.

Intrusion Detection Systems (IDS)

An IDS monitors network and system traffic for suspicious activity and issues alerts when such activity is detected. The primary function of an IDS is to serve as a digital watch guard, analyzing copies of the traffic and comparing them against a database of known threat signatures using **Signature-Based Detection** by comparing signatures of known threats against observed events to identify matches, or anomalous behavior patterns using **Anomaly-Based Detection** by establishing a baseline of normal network behavior and flags deviations, which might indicate a potential security threat. Some of the more advanced systems would use a **Hybrid Approach** which is a combination of both approach for more comprehensive monitoring.

Intrusion Prevention Systems (IPS)

An IPS, often considered an extension of an IDS, not only detects potential threats but also takes pre-defined actions to prevent the threat from causing harm. It sits directly in the line of network traffic, allowing it to block malicious activity in real time.

Once a potential threat is detected, the IPS can take immediate action, such as blocking traffic from a malicious IP address, terminating a harmful connection, or quarantining infected files.

Many modern IPS solutions are integrated with firewalls to provide both detection and prevention capabilities, leveraging deep packet inspection to analyze and take action on traffic. There are performance trade-offs with integrated solutions and security architects need to take this into any design decisions.

Evolution of IDS/IPS

Initially, IDS solutions were developed to supplement traditional firewalls by providing a deeper analysis of network traffic for malicious activities that might slip through firewall rules. As cyber threats evolved, IDS/IPS technologies advanced to incorporate sophisticated detection methods, including machine learning algorithms for anomaly detection and threat prediction.

The integration of IDS/IPS with other network security solutions, such as firewalls and endpoint security, led to the development of unified security platforms. This integration enhances the overall security posture by providing a layered defense strategy. With the advent of cloud computing and the decentralization of network environments, IDS/IPS systems have adapted to secure not just the network perimeter but also to provide in-depth security across cloud services, endpoints, and mobile devices.

Modern IDS/IPS systems increasingly rely on behavioral analysis and artificial intelligence to predict and identify zero-day exploits and sophisticated multi-stage attacks that do not match any known signatures.

The evolution of cloud computing has led to the development of cloud-native and virtual IDS/IPS solutions, designed to secure virtualized environments and cloud services with the same level of efficacy as on-premise networks.

IDS/IPS technologies have become more sophisticated and integral to comprehensive network security strategies. Their evolution reflects the changing nature of cyber threats and the increasing complexity of network environments. By continuously adapting and integrating with other security technologies, IDS/IPS systems remain crucial for detecting and preventing intrusions, ensuring the resilience of modern digital infrastructures against cyber attacks.

Network Access Control (NAC)

NAC is a security solution that enforces policy compliance on devices seeking to access network resources, thereby ensuring that only compliant and authenticated devices can access the network. NAC systems are designed to protect networks by combining endpoint security management, user or system authentication, and network security enforcement.

The primary concept behind NAC is to prevent unauthorized access to the network and to ensure that all devices connected to the network are compliant with the organization's security policies. This includes ensuring that devices have the appropriate security updates, configurations, and other protections in place.

Initially, when a device tries to connect to the network, the NAC system identifies and authenticates the device and its user. This can involve checking user credentials and the device's identity through certificates or other methods.

Once authenticated, the device's security posture is assessed. This includes checking for required software updates, antivirus signatures, and system configurations against the organization's security policies.

Based on the assessment, the NAC system decides whether to allow access, deny access, or grant limited access to the network. Devices that do not meet the security standards may be directed to a remediation network where they can update their settings or software to comply with policy requirements.

NAC systems also continuously monitor connected devices to ensure they remain compliant with security policies during their network session. If a device falls out of compliance, the system can automatically reassess and adjust the device's network access.

Evolution of NAC

Early NAC solutions were primarily focused on controlling access through pre-admission endpoint health checks. These were often cumbersome to implement and manage, especially in large and diverse network environments.

As the concept of NAC evolved, it began to integrate more closely with other security solutions, such as intrusion prevention systems (IPS), firewalls, and security information and event management (SIEM) systems. This integration allowed for more dynamic responses to security threats and improved overall network visibility.

The rise of mobile devices, BYOD (Bring Your Own Device) policies, and cloud computing required NAC solutions to adapt. Modern NAC systems support a wider range of devices and can enforce policies in both on-premises and cloud environments. Advanced NAC systems now incorporate machine learning and artificial intelligence to better identify patterns, assess risks, and automate responses. This has improved the efficiency and effectiveness of NAC systems in detecting and responding to threats.

Recent developments in NAC technology emphasize not just the security posture of devices but also the behavior of users and devices on the network. This includes monitoring for abnormal activities that could indicate a security threat. NAC is increasingly seen as a component of the Zero Trust security model, which assumes no inherent trust in any entity, whether inside or outside the network perimeter. NAC systems are evolving to support Zero Trust architectures by enforcing strict access controls and continuously verifying the security status of devices and users.

The evolution of NAC reflects broader changes in technology and security landscapes. As networks become more complex and threats more sophisticated, NAC has grown from a simple access control tool to a sophisticated security solution capable of dynamic policy enforcement, integration with broader security ecosystems, and support for diverse and decentralized network environments.

Packet Capture Tools

Packet capture tools are essential components of network security and analysis, providing the functionality to intercept and log traffic that passes over a digital network. By capturing and inspecting packets, these tools offer invaluable insights into the data flow, allowing network administrators and security professionals to monitor network activity, diagnose issues, analyze traffic patterns, and detect malicious behavior.

Packet capture tools work by intercepting network packets at various points within the network infrastructure. This can be done using a software application running on a network host or a dedicated hardware device tapped into network links. The tools use network interfaces in promiscuous mode to capture all packets on the network segment they are attached to, not just those addressed to them. After capturing the packets, the tools store the data for further analysis. This can involve saving the packets to a file or database. High-performance packet capture solutions are designed to handle large volumes of data, capturing and storing terabytes of packet data efficiently. Captured packets can be analyzed in real-time or from stored data. Analysis might include examining packet headers and payloads to understand the types of protocols being used, the source and destination of packets, and the content of the data being transmitted. Advanced analysis can help identify patterns indicative of cyber threats, such as malware communication, unauthorized data exfiltration, or network scanning activities.

Packet capture tools often include reporting features that summarize the analysis findings, providing dashboards and alerts that can notify administrators of potential security issues, network performance problems, or compliance violations.

Evolution of Packet Capture Tools

Initially, packet capture tools were simple, command-line utilities like "Tcpdump". These tools were primarily used for troubleshooting network issues, offering basic capabilities to capture and display packet information. Over time, more sophisticated tools like "Wireshark" evolved, providing graphical interfaces and more advanced packet analysis features. These tools allowed for more detailed inspection of packet contents, including the ability to decode and interpret various network protocols.

As network speeds and volumes of traffic increased, packet capture tools advanced to keep pace. This involved improvements in capture speed, storage efficiency, and the ability to perform real-time analysis on high-speed networks. Hardware-based packet capture solutions also emerged, offering dedicated processing power to handle packet capturing and analysis without impacting network performance.

With the rise in cyber threats, the focus of packet capture tools expanded from network troubleshooting to include security analysis. Tools began to integrate with intrusion detection systems (IDS) and security information and event management (SIEM) systems, providing detailed data for detecting and investigating security incidents. Recent developments in packet capture tools include the integration of automation and machine learning algorithms. These advancements help in automatically identifying patterns and anomalies that could indicate sophisticated cyber attacks, reducing the need for manual analysis and speeding up response times. Modern packet capture tools have adapted to cloud and virtualized network environments. They can capture traffic in virtualized infrastructure and cloud services, providing visibility into these increasingly common components of enterprise networks.

Packet capture tools are a vital part of network security, offering the detailed data necessary for comprehensive network visibility, troubleshooting, security monitoring, and forensic analysis. Their evolution reflects the growing complexity of networks and the increasing sophistication of cyber threats, underscoring their importance in maintaining secure and reliable network operations.

NetFlow Capture

Another tool to help with network security is NetFlow analysis. NetFlow is a network protocol developed by Cisco Systems that collects IP network traffic as it enters or exits an interface. By analyzing the flow of data, NetFlow provides valuable insights into network traffic patterns and volume, which can be used for various purposes, including network performance monitoring, planning, and, crucially, enhancing network security.

NetFlow operates by collecting data about IP flows, which are essentially sequences of packets sharing common attributes such as the source IP address, destination IP address, source port, destination port, and the protocol type. When a packet arrives at a router or switch, the device examines the packet's header to determine if it belongs to a current flow. If it does, NetFlow updates the statistics for that flow; otherwise, it creates a new flow record. The flow data collected includes details about the flow's source, destination, total packets, total bytes, start and end timestamps, and more. This information is periodically exported from the router or switch to a centralized NetFlow collector and analyzer for processing.

By continuously monitoring network traffic patterns, NetFlow can help identify anomalies that may indicate malicious activities, such as Distributed Denial of Service (DDoS) attacks, network scans, or unexpected surges in traffic to certain destinations. Anomalies are detected by comparing current traffic patterns against historical baselines to spot significant deviations.

In the event of a security incident, NetFlow data can be used to reconstruct the sequence of events leading up to the incident. This can help identify the source of an attack, the method used, and the extent of the impact. NetFlow records provide a historical account of network traffic, which is invaluable for forensic investigations.

NetFlow can also assist in monitoring compliance with network security policies by providing visibility into the types of traffic flowing through the network. It can help ensure that only authorized applications and services are being used and identify potential policy violations. By analyzing traffic flows, NetFlow can identify unauthorized use of network resources or bandwidth hogging applications, which could compromise network performance and security. It enables administrators to enforce bandwidth policies and ensure that critical services have the necessary resources. NetFlow provides comprehensive visibility into network activity, helping administrators understand how the network is being used and by whom. This visibility is crucial for detecting stealthy threats that may not trigger traditional security mechanisms but can still pose significant risks.

While NetFlow was originally a Cisco proprietary protocol, it has since become a de facto industry standard, with many other network equipment manufacturers supporting NetFlow or similar flow-based technologies (e.g., sFlow, J-Flow). The protocol itself has evolved, with versions such as NetFlow v9 and IPFIX (Internet Protocol Flow Information Export) adding enhanced capabilities, including support for flexible and extensible data models that can capture a wider range of packet attributes.

IPFIX, considered the standard version of NetFlow, extends the protocol's utility beyond Cisco devices, allowing for interoperability across different vendors' equipment and providing a universal standard for collecting and analyzing flow data.

NetFlow and its derivatives play a critical role in enhancing network security by providing detailed insights into network traffic patterns and behaviors. This capability enables organizations to detect and respond to security threats more effectively, conduct detailed forensic analyses, and maintain comprehensive visibility into network activities.

Network Visibility Tools

Network visibility tools are essential for maintaining a secure, efficient, and reliable network. These tools provide a comprehensive view into all aspects of network traffic, enabling organizations to monitor, analyze, and respond to potential security threats and performance issues. As networks have grown in complexity, with the proliferation of cloud services, mobile devices, and the Internet of Things (IoT), the role of network visibility tools has become increasingly critical.

Network visibility tools collect data from various points within a network, including routers, switches, firewalls, and other network devices. They use technologies such as packet capture, NetFlow/IPFIX, SNMP, and log files to gather information about the traffic flowing through the network. This data is then aggregated, analyzed, and presented in a usable format through dashboards, alerts, and reports.

These tools can help in identifying the types of traffic on the network, including applications, protocols, and services being used. This helps in understanding network usage patterns and identifying unauthorized or malicious activity. Using advanced analytics, including behavioral analysis and signature-based detection, they can be used to identify potential security threats such as malware infections, data exfiltration attempts, and unauthorized access.

Post incident, they can also help with forensics and troubleshooting by providing detailed historical data that can be used to investigate security incidents or network problems after they occur, helping to determine the cause and prevent future occurrences.

Early network visibility was limited to basic monitoring tools that used Simple Network Management Protocol (SNMP) to collect metrics from network devices. These tools were primarily focused on performance monitoring, with limited capabilities for traffic analysis or security.

As technology evolved, newer technologies such as NetFlow and sFlow began to provide more detailed insights into the types of traffic flowing through the network. This allowed for better capacity planning, traffic shaping, and the early stages of security analysis. The advent of packet capture technology marked a significant evolution, enabling the detailed inspection of individual data packets.

As cyber threats increased, network visibility tools began to incorporate more sophisticated security features. This included the integration with Intrusion Detection Systems (IDS), Intrusion Prevention Systems (IPS), and later, advanced threat detection capabilities using machine learning and artificial intelligence.

The latest evolution in network visibility tools has seen the consolidation of monitoring, analysis, and security functions into unified platforms. These platforms offer comprehensive visibility across the entire network infrastructure, combining data from multiple sources to provide a holistic view of network health, performance, and security.

Network visibility tools play a crucial role in network security by providing the insights needed to detect and respond to potential threats, ensure compliance, and optimize network performance. As networks continue to evolve in complexity and scope, these tools will remain indispensable for securing and managing modern network environments.

Security Policy Enforcement

Technology alone does not help with improving the security of the network. Security policy enforcement is a critical aspect of an organization's overall security posture, ensuring that policies designed to protect assets and data are effectively applied and adhered to across the organization. Enforcement can be achieved through a combination of real-time technology, passive technology-assisted compliance checks, non-technical compliance measures, and contractual compliance checks. Each of these approaches plays a vital role in maintaining a secure and compliant operational environment.

Real-Time Technology Enforcement	Passive Tech-assisted Compliance
Firewalls/Intrusion Prevention Systems DLP Solutions Access Control Systems Endpoint Protection	Intrusion Detection System Log Analysis Vulnerability Scanner Configuration Management
Non-technical Compliance	**Contractual Compliance**
Security Audit Employee Training and Awareness Policy Reviews and Updates	Security Clauses in Contracts Third Party Assessment Regular External Audit Reporting

Real-Time Technology Enforcement

Real-time technology enforcement involves using automated systems and tools to enforce security policies immediately as data flows through the network or when users interact with systems. This proactive approach relies on various technologies, including:

Firewalls and Intrusion Prevention Systems (IPS): Automatically block unauthorized access and malicious traffic based on predefined security policies.

Data Loss Prevention (DLP) Solutions: Monitor and control data transfer to prevent sensitive information from leaving the network without authorization.

Access Control Systems: Enforce policies regarding who can access specific resources within the network, ensuring users only have access to the data and systems necessary for their role.

Endpoint Protection Platforms: Ensure that devices comply with security policies through real-time monitoring and enforcement, such as requiring up-to-date antivirus software and applying necessary security patches.

These technologies enable organizations to enforce security policies dynamically, reducing the risk of security breaches and ensuring compliance with regulatory standards.

Passive Technology-Assisted Compliance Check

Passive technology-assisted compliance checks involve monitoring and auditing systems and networks to verify compliance with security policies without actively intervening in data flows or system operations. This approach includes:

Log Management and Analysis Tools: Collect and analyze logs from various systems and devices to identify potential security policy violations or suspicious activities.

Vulnerability Scanners: Periodically scan systems and networks for vulnerabilities that could violate security policies, providing reports that guide remediation efforts.

Configuration Management Tools: Assess systems and devices to ensure they are configured according to organizational security policies, identifying deviations for correction.

Passive checks are essential for identifying areas where security policies may not be effectively enforced, allowing organizations to make informed decisions about where to focus their security efforts.

Non-Technical Compliance Check

Non-technical compliance checks involve processes and procedures that are not based on technology solutions but rather on organizational policies and human activities. These include:

Security Audits and Assessments: Regularly scheduled audits performed by internal or external parties to evaluate adherence to security policies and identify areas for improvement.

Employee Training and Awareness Programs: Educating employees about security policies and their importance to ensure understanding and compliance.

Policy Review and Update Processes: Regularly reviewing and updating security policies to reflect changes in the threat landscape, business processes, or regulatory requirements.

These checks are crucial for creating a culture of security within the organization and ensuring that all employees understand and adhere to security policies.

Contractual Compliance Check

Contractual compliance checks ensure that third parties, such as vendors, partners, and contractors, comply with the organization's security policies as part of their contractual obligations. This involves:

Security Clauses in Contracts: Including specific security requirements and compliance obligations in contracts with third parties.

Third-Party Assessments: Conducting security assessments or requiring third-party certifications (e.g., ISO 27001, SOC 2) to verify that partners and vendors meet the organization's security standards.

Regular Reporting and Audit Rights: Requiring third parties to provide regular security compliance reports and allowing the organization to audit third-party compliance as necessary.

Contractual compliance checks help manage the risk associated with third-party relationships, ensuring that external entities handling the organization's data or systems adhere to its security policies.

Effective security policy enforcement requires a multifaceted approach that combines real-time technology enforcement, passive compliance checks, non-technical measures, and contractual obligations. When paired with the right technology solution, these strategies ensure comprehensive compliance with security policies, safeguarding the organization's assets and data against evolving threats.

Endpoint Security

Endpoint security is a critical component in an organization's overall cybersecurity strategy, aimed at protecting endpoints—such as desktops, laptops, and mobile devices—from a myriad of cyber threats. These endpoints serve as access points to an organization's network and are often targeted by attackers to gain entry and execute malicious activities. The evolution of endpoint security solutions, from basic antivirus software to advanced Endpoint Detection and Response (EDR) systems, showcases the cybersecurity industry's response to the ever-evolving threat landscape. For purpose of this book, the endpoint protection landscape would be classified into three categories - Basic, Advanced, and Next Generation.

Basic	Advanced	Next-Generation
Anti-Virus	Signature based EDR	Deep Learning EDR
Application whitelisting	Data Lost Protection	
Device Whitelisting		

Basic Endpoint Protection

At the most basic level of endpoint security are anti-virus programs. These solutions are designed to detect, quarantine, and remove malicious software (malware) based on known signatures. Signatures are unique strings or patterns that identify specific malware, allowing anti-virus software to recognize and block threats that have been previously identified and analyzed. While effective against known threats, the reliance on signatures is also a limitation; new, unknown (zero-day) threats can easily bypass traditional anti-virus solutions.

Other basic endpoint security practice includes application whitelisting and device whitelisting which represents a targeted approaches within the spectrum of endpoint protection strategies. These methodologies focus on allowing only verified, trusted software or devices to operate within an IT environment, thereby providing a proactive defense mechanism against malware, unauthorized applications, and external device threats.

Application whitelisting is a security measure that permits only pre-approved software applications to run on a system or network. Unlike traditional antivirus solutions that block known malicious programs, application whitelisting allows only specified applications to execute, automatically denying all others.

In this case, administrators create a whitelist, or a list of approved software, based on the specific needs and security policies of the organization. The endpoint security system monitors attempts to execute software on the device. If the software is not on the whitelist, it is prevented from running. This approach significantly reduces the risk of malware infections since only known and trusted applications can execute.

While this approach provides a strong protection against zero-day attacks, as unknown programs (which could be malicious) are not allowed to run and it reduces the system's attack surface by limiting the number of applications that could potentially be exploited, application whitelisting requires careful management and updating of the whitelist to ensure that legitimate software updates and new applications are not inadvertently blocked. This can prove to be labor-intensive to implement and maintain, particularly in environments with diverse software requirements.

Device whitelisting secures endpoints by only allowing pre-approved devices to connect to a system or network. This could include USB drives, external hard drives, smartphones, and other peripheral devices. Similar to application whitelisting, administrators compile a list of approved devices based on unique identifiers (such as serial numbers or MAC addresses). Only devices on the whitelist are permitted to connect and interact with the system. Unauthorized devices are blocked from establishing a connection. This approach can protects against data leakage by preventing unauthorized devices from accessing the network and copying sensitive information and reduces the risk of malware introduction through infected external devices.

Like application whitelisting, device whitelisting requires ongoing management to accommodate new and legitimate devices and may inadvertently disrupt workflow if legitimate devices are not promptly whitelisted, impacting productivity.

Advanced Endpoint Protection

To combat the limitations of signature-based detection, heuristic analysis techniques were developed. These techniques analyze the behavior of programs to detect suspicious activity that deviates from normal operations, potentially indicating malware. Heuristic analysis can identify new malware variants and unknown threats by focusing on behavior rather than signatures.

Endpoint Protection Platforms (EPP) solutions represent an evolution in endpoint security, offering a more comprehensive approach. These platforms combine traditional anti-virus capabilities with heuristic analysis, firewall management, email filtering, and more. EPP solutions are designed to prevent threats using a multi-layered approach, providing a broader range of protection mechanisms to address various attack vectors.

Endpoint Detection and Response (EDR) systems take endpoint security a step further by focusing not just on prevention, but also on detection and response. EDR solutions continuously monitor endpoints for malicious activities and anomalies, offering capabilities to investigate threats, perform forensic analysis, and respond to incidents. EDR tools provide detailed visibility into endpoint activities, allowing security teams to quickly understand the scope of an attack and effectively contain and remediate incidents.

Signature-Based EDR combine the traditional signature-based approach with behavioral analysis, providing a robust mechanism to detect known and emerging threats. Signature-based EDR solutions can quickly identify and block known malware, while also employing behavioral heuristics to uncover suspicious activities that may indicate a novel attack.

Next Generation Endpoint Protection

With technological advances, next generation EDR solutions incorporate signature-based detection with cutting-edge technologies like deep learning and artificial intelligence (AI) to enhance their effectiveness.

Deep learning EDR solutions utilize AI algorithms to analyze massive datasets and learn from them, identifying patterns and anomalies that would be impossible for humans to detect manually. This approach allows for the identification of sophisticated, previously unseen threats by understanding the normal behavior of systems and users, and detecting deviations that could indicate a compromise. Deep learning techniques enable proactive threat hunting and more effective response strategies, significantly improving the detection of zero-day exploits and advanced persistent threats (APTs).

The evolution from basic anti-virus to advanced EDR solutions equipped with deep learning capabilities illustrates the cybersecurity industry's adaptive response to the growing sophistication of cyber threats. As attackers employ more advanced techniques, endpoint security solutions continue to evolve, leveraging the latest technologies to provide comprehensive protection, detection, and response capabilities, ensuring that organizations can defend their networks and sensitive data against an ever-changing threat landscape.

The Cyber Kill Chain

The Cyber Kill Chain framework, developed by Lockheed Martin, describes the stages of a cyber attack from early reconnaissance to the final act of data exfiltration or system compromise. We can plan our endpoint protection strategy using this framework as a guide.

The framework consists of seven stages: reconnaissance, weaponization, delivery, exploitation, installation, command and control (C2), and actions on objectives. Each of these stages presents opportunities for defending against an attack, especially when focusing on endpoint protection. The attack can be disrupted at any of the stage to prevent a successful infiltration from the attacker.

Stage 1: Reconnaissance

In this initial phase, attackers gather information about the target. Endpoint protection can mitigate risks by limiting the amount of publicly available information on endpoint configurations and network architecture. This can be done by using endpoint protection solutions that include threat intelligence to identify and block reconnaissance activities.

Stage 2: Weaponization

During this stage, attackers create malware tailored to target identified vulnerabilities. Endpoint protection strategies need to include regularly updating and patching endpoints to close vulnerabilities that could be exploited. Another option is to implement advanced endpoint protection platforms (EPPs) that can detect and block known and unknown malware.

Stage 3: Delivery

During this stage, the malware is delivered to the target, commonly through email phishing, websites, or direct network access. To protect endpoints, the common strategies include deploying email security solutions that scan attachments and links for threats; the use of web filters to prevent access to malicious sites; and to employ endpoint protection solutions that can automatically quarantine suspicious files.

Stage 4: Exploitation

In this stage, the malware exploits a vulnerability to execute on the target endpoint. Endpoint protection measures for this includes employing EDR solutions that can detect exploitation attempts in real-time, and ensuring all software on endpoints is kept up-to-date to minimize vulnerabilities.

Stage 5: Installation

In this stage, malware installs itself on the target system to maintain persistence. Endpoint protection can counteract this by utilizing application whitelisting to prevent unauthorized applications from installing. Another action is to leverage EDR tools that monitor for changes in the system indicative of malware installation.

Stage 6: Command and Control (C2)

Here, the malware communicates back to the attacker's server to receive further instructions. Endpoint protection efforts involve outgoing firewalls at the endpoint that monitor outbound connections for C2 activity. Endpoint solutions with behavioral analysis capabilities to detect and block unauthorized communication attempts can also be deployed.

Stage 7: Actions on Objectives

In the final stage, attackers execute their intended actions, such as data exfiltration, encryption for ransom, or system disruption. To defend endpoints, one method is the deployment of data loss prevention (DLP) technologies to monitor and restrict unauthorized data transfers, or to implement endpoint solutions with capabilities to rollback changes made by ransomware.

Integrating the Cyber Kill Chain framework into endpoint protection strategies involves a layered defense approach that addresses vulnerabilities at each stage of an attack. This includes deploying a mix of traditional antivirus, EPP, and EDR solutions, coupled with security best practices such as regular patching, user education, and the principle of least privilege. By understanding the attacker's methods and tactics at each phase of the kill chain, security teams can tailor their endpoint protection measures to more effectively detect, prevent, and respond to cyber threats, thus breaking the chain before attackers can achieve their objectives.

Identity and Access Management

Identity and Access Management (IAM) stands as a foundational pillar in the architecture of enterprise security, orchestrating the delicate balance between ensuring seamless access to resources and safeguarding sensitive information from unauthorized eyes. At its core, IAM encompasses the methodologies, policies, and technologies dedicated to managing digital identities and meticulously controlling how these identities are authenticated, authorized, and audited across organizational systems.

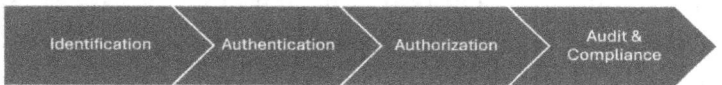

The process begins with the identification of users through unique credentials, followed by authentication via various means such as passwords, biometrics, or multi-factor authentication (MFA), to verify the user's claim to the identity. Once authenticated, the system determines the extent of the user's access, delineating what resources can be accessed and the actions permitted, based on pre-established policies. Integral to IAM is also the capability to monitor and log access events, an essential feature for adhering to compliance mandates and performing security audits.

The architecture of IAM is built on several key components including Directory Services, which act as central repositories for user information; Single Sign-On (SSO), which facilitates access to multiple systems with a single authentication event; Multi-Factor Authentication (MFA), adding an extra layer of security; Role-Based Access Control (RBAC), simplifying permission management by assigning access rights based on organizational roles; Privileged Access Management (PAM), focusing on the oversight of high-level accounts; and Identity Federation, which enables the sharing of identity information across varied security domains.

Organizations have the flexibility to deploy IAM systems in different environments: on-premises, which offers complete control over the IAM infrastructure; cloud-based, also known as Identity as a Service (IDaaS), which provides scalability and reduced overhead; or a hybrid approach, blending both on-premises and cloud-based solutions to cater to specific organizational needs or regulatory requirements.

IAM's significance in enterprise security cannot be overstated. It not only fortifies the barriers against unauthorized access but also ensures that regulatory compliance is seamlessly integrated into daily operations. Moreover, by streamlining the management of access rights, IAM systems enhance organizational efficiency and productivity, ensuring that employees have timely access to the necessary resources. Furthermore, IAM plays a critical role in risk management, mitigating the potential for insider threats and breaches that could arise from compromised credentials. In the ever-evolving landscape of digital threats and expanding digital footprints, the implementation of a robust IAM strategy is indispensable for organizations aiming to protect their critical assets while maintaining operational integrity and compliance with regulatory standards.

IAM Tools

As IAM is an encompassing framework designed to ensure that the right individuals gain access to the appropriate resources at the right times for the right reasons. It encompasses various tools and processes that help in managing identities within an organization, as well as managing their access to different resources. Diving deeper, IAM can be divided into two main components: Identity Management and Access Management. Each plays a vital role in the security and efficiency of IT environments.

Identity Management

Identity Management focuses on the administrative actions related to identifying individuals within a system and controlling their access to resources through identity-based policies. This includes tasks such as creating new user accounts, managing user attributes, provisioning and de-provisioning users, and managing passwords. The goal is to ensure that every individual has a unique digital identity that can be accurately associated with them.

Tools for IM are usually around the following functions:

User Provisioning: Automates the creation, modification, and deletion of user accounts across various systems and platforms.

Directory Services: Act as repositories for storing and managing digital identities, like LDAP (Lightweight Directory Access Protocol) directories and Active Directory.

Password Management: Provides mechanisms for users to manage their passwords securely, including resets and complexity requirements.

Multi-Factor Authentication (MFA): Adds an extra layer of security by requiring users to verify their identity using two or more verification methods before gaining access.

Identity Federation: Allows identities to be used across multiple systems, reducing the need for multiple usernames and passwords.

Access Management

Access Management, on the other hand, deals with managing access rights and permissions for those identities. This involves determining which resources a user can access within a network and what actions they are permitted to perform with those resources. It's about matching user rights and restrictions with the roles they hold within an organization.

Tools for AM are for the following functions:

Single Sign-On (SSO): Enables users to access multiple applications with one set of credentials, improving user experience while maintaining security.

Role-Based Access Control (RBAC): Access rights are granted according to the role of a user within an organization, simplifying the management of user permissions.

Access Reviews and Certifications: Regular audits of user access to ensure compliance with security policies and regulations.

Difference between IAM and IGA

While IAM encompasses the broad scope of managing identities and their access, Identity Governance and Administration (IGA) focuses more on the governance aspect, ensuring that access rights are compliant with policy and regulatory requirements. IGA provides a framework for policy management, role management, compliance management, and audit management. It is concerned with answering questions like "Should this user have access to this resource?" and "Is this access aligned with our compliance requirements?"

IAM is more operationally focused, emphasizing the efficiency and security of access management and identity management processes. While IGA adds a layer of governance, focusing on ensuring that access rights are appropriately managed, monitored, and reported according to compliance and business policies.

In summary, while Identity Management sets up the digital identities and manages their lifecycle, Access Management controls what resources and operations the identities can access. Both are critical components of IAM, ensuring that only authorized individuals can access the necessary resources efficiently and securely. IGA, as an extension, brings in the governance aspect, making sure that these processes align with broader organizational policies and compliance requirements.

Application Security

Application security, within the realm of enterprise security, refers to the measures and processes designed to protect applications from threats and vulnerabilities throughout their lifecycle, from design and development to deployment and maintenance. This critical component of enterprise security encompasses a broad range of practices aimed at securing all aspects of application usage and development against exploitation by attackers. Central to application security is the concept of "shifting left," which involves integrating security measures early in the software development life cycle (SDLC) to identify and mitigate vulnerabilities before deployment. For the purpose of this book, the various aspects are put into 6 categories - Code security, system security, availability, data bases, Operating Systems Security, cloud-native security.

Code	System	Availability
White Box Testing	Black Box Testing	Load Testing
Peer Review	Penetration Testing	Performance Testing
Requirements to Code	Application Firewalls	Dependent systems

Databases	OS Security	Cloud Native
DB Activity monitoring	Isolation (Namespaces)	Containers
Limited Access Channels	Control Groups	Serverless Apps
Manage Configuration	Secure Computing Mode	Cloud native Services

Code Security

Code scanning and review are foundational practices in application security. Automated tools, alongside manual review processes, scrutinize the source code for common security issues such as injection flaws, cross-site scripting (XSS), and other vulnerabilities that could be exploited by attackers. These practices ensure that code is examined for potential security risks, with the aim of fixing issues before the application is deployed. This is known as "White Box" testing as you have access to the code and can do a low level review of the security in the code.

In more secure environment (like the space program or military systems). There is even a need to trace every line of code back to a requirement. This is done to ensure no extra functions are added to the base application by developers.

System Security

To complement white box testing, we have also the concept of "black Box" testing. Black box testing, also known as behavioral testing, is an approach where the tester evaluates the application without any prior knowledge of its internal workings, infrastructure, or code. Testers interact with the application's external interfaces—such as web APIs, user interfaces, and endpoints—to uncover security vulnerabilities that could be exploited by an attacker. This method simulates an external attack or the perspective of an end-user to identify security flaws that are visible from outside the system. This is usually performed while the application is running, allowing testers to understand how the application responds to various inputs and actions.

Black box testing is particularly effective for detecting issues related to input validation, session management, and cross-site scripting (XSS), among others. It's a critical component of application security as it highlights vulnerabilities that could be exploited by attackers without internal knowledge of the system.

Penetration testing, or pen testing, is a simulated cyber attack against your computer system to check for exploitable vulnerabilities. In the context of application security, penetration testing is a more comprehensive approach that may encompass both black box and white (or clear) box strategies to assess the security of an application. Pen testers may start with limited knowledge about the application (similar to black box testing) but often use additional information about the system's configuration, code, and architecture (akin to white box testing) to perform a thorough security assessment.

Penetration testing usually goes beyond testing the application's external interfaces and may include source code analysis, infrastructure testing, and internal network access to identify vulnerabilities across the entire application ecosystem. It mimics the actions of both unskilled attackers and knowledgeable hackers to identify potential security breaches.

Penetration testing is essential for uncovering complex security vulnerabilities that may not be detected through automated scans or black box testing alone. It provides a deeper understanding of potential security threats and helps organizations prioritize remediation efforts based on the severity and exploitability of identified vulnerabilities.

Both black box testing and penetration testing play vital roles in the field of application security, offering unique insights into an application's vulnerability landscape. While black box testing offers an attacker's perspective with no prior knowledge of the system, penetration testing provides a comprehensive assessment of potential security weaknesses, including those that require insider knowledge to exploit. Together, these testing methodologies help organizations strengthen their application security posture and protect against potential cyber threats.

Availability

In the context of security architecture, testing for availability is as crucial as safeguarding against unauthorized access or data breaches. The cornerstone of a robust security strategy is not only to prevent attacks but also to ensure that systems remain accessible and performant under various conditions. This involves a comprehensive approach that encompasses load testing, performance testing, and the analysis of dependent systems.

Load testing is essential for understanding how systems behave under high demand. By simulating a significant number of simultaneous users or requests, organizations can identify potential bottlenecks or failures that could lead to downtime, ensuring that the system can handle expected traffic volumes without compromising service quality. This is particularly important in scenarios where service availability is critical, such as in financial transactions or emergency response systems.

Performance testing goes hand-in-hand with load testing, focusing on how the system performs under typical and peak load conditions. It helps in identifying the limits of an application in terms of response time and resource utilization, ensuring that performance thresholds meet the operational requirements. Performance testing is crucial for maintaining user satisfaction and for the smooth operation of business processes, as delays and sluggish response times can lead to frustration, reduced productivity, and loss of revenue.

The **analysis of dependent system**s is another critical aspect of ensuring availability. In today's interconnected environments, the functionality of one system often relies on the availability and performance of another. A comprehensive security architecture must therefore include an evaluation of these dependencies to identify potential points of failure that could impact overall system availability. This involves mapping out the network of interdependencies and understanding how issues in one area can ripple through to others, potentially bringing critical functions to a halt.

Testing for availability is a vital component of security architecture that ensures systems are resilient, reliable, and capable of meeting user demands even under stress. By incorporating load testing, performance testing, and dependent systems analysis into their security practices, organizations can not only protect their assets from attacks but also from the potentially equally damaging effects of downtime and poor performance. This holistic view of security underscores the importance of availability alongside confidentiality and integrity in maintaining the trust and confidence of users and stakeholders in digital systems.

Database Security

Database security is a critical aspect of protecting sensitive information within an organization, encompassing a wide range of practices and tools designed to safeguard databases against compromises and unauthorized access. Given the value and sensitivity of the data stored in databases—ranging from personal customer information to proprietary business intelligence—ensuring their security is paramount. Key strategies in database security include the use of database activity monitoring tools, implementing limited access channels, and rigorous configuration management.

Database Activity Monitoring (DAM) tools are essential for real-time monitoring, alerting, and reporting on database activities. They track and analyze all access and operations performed on the data, including queries, updates, and schema changes, regardless of whether these actions originate from within the organization or from external sources. By doing so, DAM tools help in identifying unusual or unauthorized activities that could indicate a security breach, such as excessive login attempts, unusual data access patterns, or attempts to access sensitive data outside of normal business hours. These tools can also enforce policies, block suspicious activities, and provide detailed audit trails for compliance purposes.

Another technique is to implement **"Limited Access Channels"**. Restricting access to databases is fundamental to their security. This involves defining and enforcing strict access controls that limit who can view or modify data. Access should be based on the principle of least privilege, ensuring that individuals have only the permissions necessary to perform their job functions. This minimizes the risk of accidental or deliberate misuse of data. Furthermore, access channels themselves can be secured by implementing network segmentation, creating dedicated pathways for database access that are isolated from the rest of the network to reduce the risk of lateral movement by attackers. An example of this could be access to the database can only be from the application and not from an interactive console.

Proper **configuration management** is crucial in securing databases against vulnerabilities. This includes regularly updating database management systems (DBMS) to patch known vulnerabilities, removing unnecessary features or services that could introduce security risks, and configuring database settings to enforce strong authentication, encryption, and logging practices. Regularly reviewing and updating configurations to align with best security practices helps in mitigating potential attack vectors and reduces the overall risk profile of database systems. In addition to these strategies, encrypting data at rest and in transit provides a strong layer of protection by ensuring that even if data is intercepted or accessed by unauthorized individuals, it remains unreadable without the proper decryption keys. Similarly, regularly backing up data and testing recovery procedures are vital to maintaining data integrity and availability in the event of a breach or data loss.

Database security is a multifaceted discipline that requires a comprehensive approach to protect sensitive information from a wide range of threats. By employing database activity monitoring tools, implementing limited access channels, and adhering to rigorous configuration management practices, organizations can significantly enhance the security of their databases. These measures, combined with encryption and regular backups, form a robust defense-in-depth strategy that helps safeguard critical data assets and ensure the ongoing confidentiality, integrity, and availability of information.

Operating Systems Security

Operating System (OS) security plays a crucial role in the broader context of application security. It provides the foundational layer of protection upon which applications operate, ensuring they do so in a secure and controlled environment. Modern operating systems offer various mechanisms and tools designed to isolate applications, limit their access to system resources, and control their ability to execute specific operations. Among these tools, namespaces, control groups (cgroups), and seccomp (Secure Computing Mode) stand out for their effectiveness in enhancing application security.

Namespaces are a feature of the Linux kernel that partitions kernel resources such that one set of processes sees one set of resources while another set of processes sees a different set of resources. The system resources within a namespace are isolated from those in other namespaces. This isolation can include aspects of the system like process IDs, network interfaces, file systems, and more. For application security, namespaces are particularly valuable because they limit the impact of a compromised application. By isolating application processes in separate namespaces, an attacker who gains control of one application is prevented from easily accessing resources or interfering with processes outside that application's namespace.

Control Groups (cgroups) further enhance security by limiting and monitoring the resources that processes can use. Cgroups allow the OS to allocate resources—such as CPU time, system memory, network bandwidth, or combinations of these resources—among user-defined groups of tasks (processes). By using cgroups, system administrators can ensure that a single application or process does not consume resources to the detriment of others, which is critical for maintaining system stability and preventing certain types of Denial of Service (DoS) attacks where an application might attempt to exhaust system resources.

Secure Computing Mode (seccomp) is another powerful Linux kernel feature that restricts the system calls applications can make, effectively reducing the kernel's attack surface that an application can exploit. With seccomp, applications are forced into a state where they can only perform a minimal set of predefined system calls. Any attempt to make a system call not allowed by the seccomp policy results in the application being safely terminated. This can significantly mitigate the impact of security vulnerabilities in applications by limiting what an attacker can do if they manage to exploit an application.

Incorporating these OS-level security mechanisms into application development and deployment strategies represents a proactive approach to securing applications. By leveraging namespaces, applications can be isolated from each other, reducing the risk of lateral movement by attackers. With cgroups, applications are prevented from monopolizing system resources, protecting the system from instability and potential DoS attacks. Seccomp policies enforce a strict set of allowed operations, substantially reducing the risk of kernel-level exploits.

Operating system security features like namespaces, cgroups, and seccomp play a pivotal role in the security of applications running on modern systems. They provide critical mechanisms for isolating applications, controlling their resource usage, and limiting their capabilities, thereby forming a fundamental part of a comprehensive application security strategy. By effectively utilizing these tools, developers and system administrators can significantly enhance the security posture of their applications and the systems on which they run.

Cloud-Native Security

Cloud-native security, within the ambit of application security, represents a paradigm shift towards securing applications that are designed and deployed in highly dynamic, scalable cloud environments. Unlike traditional security models that often focus on perimeter defense, cloud-native security emphasizes a more granular, resource-centric approach. This is crucial due to the distributed nature of cloud-native applications, which typically leverage containers, serverless computing, and a range of cloud-native services. Each of these components introduces specific security considerations and challenges.

Container Security

Containers, which encapsulate an application and its dependencies into a single runnable unit, have revolutionized application deployment by ensuring consistency across different environments. However, their dynamic and ephemeral nature also introduces unique security challenges.

Image Security: Containers are instantiated from images, making the security of these images foundational. Ensuring images are free from vulnerabilities at the point of creation, and keeping them updated, is critical. Tools like Docker Bench for Security and Clair can scan images for known vulnerabilities.

Runtime Security: Once deployed, the behavior of containers needs to be monitored to detect and prevent runtime threats. Solutions like Falco can monitor container behavior, alerting on anomalies that might indicate a breach.

Network Segmentation: Containers often share the same host and can communicate over the network. Implementing network policies to control traffic flow between containers can prevent lateral movement by attackers.

Access Control: Ensuring that containers operate with the least privilege necessary and that access to container management APIs is tightly controlled is fundamental to preventing unauthorized access.

Serverless Security

Next we have serverless computing. Serverless computing, where developers write functions that are run by the cloud provider in response to events, abstracts away much of the infrastructure management. While this model reduces the attack surface related to the infrastructure, it also introduces specific security concerns:

Function Permissions: Functions should be granted only the permissions they need to operate (principle of least privilege). Overprivileged functions can become a significant risk if compromised.

Dependency Management: Functions often rely on external libraries, which can introduce vulnerabilities. Regular scanning and updating of dependencies are essential to mitigate this risk.

Event Injection: Serverless functions are triggered by events, which can be manipulated. Validating event data to prevent injection attacks is critical.

Secure Secrets Management: Serverless functions often need secrets (e.g., database passwords) to operate. These should be securely managed using cloud-native secrets management services rather than hard-coded into function code.

Security of Cloud-Native Services

Beyond containers and serverless, cloud-native applications often leverage a plethora of managed services like databases, messaging queues, and machine learning APIs. Securing these services involves many of the things mentioned earlier like ensuring data is encrypted in transit and at rest using the cloud provider's encryption capabilities to protect sensitive information; Configuring IAM policies to control access to cloud-native services is essential for maintaining a strong security posture. This includes managing roles and permissions for both human and non-human entities; Regularly auditing the configuration of cloud-native services against security benchmarks and compliance standards helps identify misconfigurations that could introduce vulnerabilities; and also utilizing cloud-native monitoring and logging services to gain visibility into application and infrastructure behavior. This data is crucial for detecting security incidents and conducting forensic analysis.

Cloud-native security requires a comprehensive and proactive approach that integrates security practices throughout the application lifecycle. From securing container images and managing serverless function permissions to ensuring robust access controls and encryption for cloud-native services, each aspect of a cloud-native application architecture demands attention. By embedding security controls and practices into the CI/CD pipeline and leveraging the security features offered by cloud providers, organizations can build and maintain secure cloud-native applications. Below is a diagram to show thew security areas of a typical CI/CD pipeline in a DevSecOps setup.

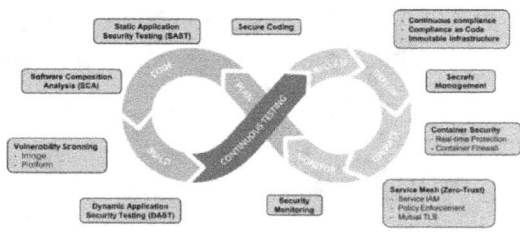

In conclusion, application security is a comprehensive discipline within enterprise security that addresses the protection of applications from threats at every stage of their development and operational life. By employing a combination of code scanning, manual review, diverse testing methodologies, database security measures, and adapting to modern deployment practices through container and cloud-native security, organizations can significantly reduce their risk profile and safeguard their critical applications from potential security breaches.

Data Protection

Data protection is another very important area in enterprise security, encompassing a wide array of techniques and technologies designed to safeguard sensitive information from unauthorized access, disclosure, or theft. In the digital era, where data breaches can have devastating consequences on an organization's reputation and financial health, implementing robust data protection measures is paramount. Among the plethora of strategies employed, anonymization, encryption, homomorphic encryption, multi-party computation, and Distributed Ledger Technology (DLT) are particularly noteworthy for their effectiveness in securing data.

Anonymization involves processing data in such a way that personal identifiers are removed or obfuscated, ensuring that individuals cannot be readily identified. This technique is crucial for protecting privacy in datasets that are used for analysis and research, allowing valuable insights to be gleaned without compromising individual privacy.

Standard encryption is the bedrock of data security, transforming readable data into an unreadable format unless one has the key to decrypt it. This ensures that even if data is intercepted or accessed by unauthorized parties, it remains indecipherable and useless to them. Encryption can be applied to data at rest, in transit, or both, providing a high level of security for sensitive information as it is stored and communicated.

Homomorphic encryption is a form of encryption that allows computations to be performed on ciphertexts, generating an encrypted result that, when decrypted, matches the result of operations performed on the plaintext. This groundbreaking approach enables secure processing of encrypted data without needing to access the original, unencrypted data. Thus, it offers a powerful tool for enhancing privacy and security in cloud computing, data analysis, and other fields where sensitive information needs to be processed without exposing it to third-party service providers or compromising the data's confidentiality. The term "homomorphic" comes from algebra, referring to a homomorphism between two algebraic structures, which is a structure-preserving map between them. In the context of encryption, this concept translates to performing operations on encrypted data (ciphertext) that preserve the structure of operations as if they were performed on the unencrypted data (plaintext). Homomorphic encryption can be broadly classified into two categories: full homomorphic encryption (FHE) and partial homomorphic encryption (PHE).

Full Homomorphic Encryption (FHE) allows for arbitrary computations on encrypted data. This means any function that can be computed on plaintext can also be computed on ciphertext without any limitations on the types of operations or the number of operations. The ability to perform unlimited computations on encrypted data makes FHE incredibly versatile and powerful, enabling a wide range of applications in secure data processing and analysis. However, FHE is computationally intensive, which has historically limited its practical applications due to the significant processing power and time required.

Partial Homomorphic Encryption (PHE), on the other hand, supports only a limited set of operations on encrypted data. For example, some PHE schemes allow for the addition of encrypted numbers but not multiplication, or vice versa. There are also schemes that support a limited number of operations before the data needs to be decrypted. PHE is less computationally demanding than FHE and has been successfully applied in various practical scenarios, such as encrypted search and secure voting systems. The limitations in the types of allowable operations, however, restrict the scope of its applications compared to FHE.

The key difference between FHE and PHE lies in the range of computations they support. While FHE offers the flexibility to perform any computation on encrypted data, making it a more universally applicable solution for secure data processing, PHE is constrained to specific types of operations. However, the trade-off is that FHE's broader capabilities come at the cost of higher computational overhead, making PHE a more practical choice for certain applications where the required operations are known in advance and fall within the PHE's capabilities.

Multi-party computation (MPC) is another innovative approach that allows multiple parties to jointly compute a function over their inputs while keeping those inputs private. Multi-party computation (MPC), also known as secure multi-party computation (SMPC or SMC), is a subfield of cryptography with the goal of creating methods for parties to jointly compute a function over their inputs while keeping those inputs private. The essence of MPC is to allow the computation of accurate results without compromising the security of each party's data, making it a powerful tool for data protection in scenarios where sharing sensitive information is a risk.

In practical terms, MPC enables different entities to collaborate on computations—such as statistical analyses, benchmarking studies, or financial transactions—without revealing their proprietary or confidential data to each other. This is achieved through cryptographic protocols that ensure the only output is the computation result, with the input data remaining obscured to all parties involved. For instance, a group of companies might want to compute the average salary of their employees without disclosing the individual salaries to avoid privacy breaches or competitive disadvantage. Through MPC, they can obtain the collective average without any party having access to the specific salary data of another.

The utility of MPC extends across various domains, including finance, healthcare, and public sector applications, where the confidentiality of data is paramount. In healthcare, for example, MPC can enable researchers to conduct collaborative studies on patient data across institutions without direct access to the patient records, thus preserving patient privacy while still contributing to medical research.

Distributed Ledger Technology (DLT), best exemplified by blockchain, offers a secure and transparent way to record transactions in a decentralized manner. DLT represents a paradigm shift in how data is stored, verified, and protected across digital platforms. At its core, DLT is a decentralized database managed by multiple participants across different locations, eliminating the need for a central authority or intermediary. This technology is most famously implemented in blockchain systems, which underpin cryptocurrencies and have broad applications ranging from financial services to supply chain management. In the context of data protection, DLT offers several unique advantages that enhance the security and integrity of information.

DLT ensures data protection through its inherent characteristics: immutability, transparency, and encryption. Once data is entered into a distributed ledger, it becomes nearly impossible to alter or delete, thanks to cryptographic hashing and the consensus mechanism required for any change in the ledger. This immutability provides a verifiable and tamper-evident record of all transactions or data entries, making DLT particularly valuable for audit trails and securing sensitive information against unauthorized modifications.

Furthermore, DLT can be configured to offer varying degrees of transparency. While all transactions are verifiable by participants, the details of those transactions can be encrypted, ensuring that sensitive information remains confidential while still benefiting from the ledger's integrity. Participants can verify that transactions occurred without seeing the actual data, a feature especially useful in scenarios requiring privacy and verification, such as in voting systems or identity management.

Encryption plays a crucial role in DLT, with data on the ledger often being encrypted to protect against unauthorized access. Advanced cryptographic techniques, including public and private key encryption, ensure that only authorized parties can access the information they are permitted to see, further bolstering data protection. The decentralized nature of DLT also means that the system does not have a single point of failure. Unlike centralized databases that can be vulnerable to cyber-attacks, the distributed architecture of DLT spreads the data across many nodes, making it exceedingly difficult for attackers to compromise the integrity or availability of the data.

DLT offers a robust framework for data protection by leveraging immutability, transparency, encryption, and decentralization. These features make DLT an attractive option for applications requiring secure, transparent, and tamper-proof systems for managing sensitive data, thereby playing a significant role in advancing data protection strategies in the digital age.

Vulnerability and Patch Management

Within enterprise security, managing vulnerabilities and ensuring effective patch management are foundational elements that protect against potential security breaches and maintain operational integrity. These practices are crucial for mitigating risks, preserving data confidentiality, integrity, and availability, and complying with regulatory standards.

Vulnerability Management	Patch Management
Intel Feeds	Test Environments
Validation Environment	Realistic Test Data
Good Communication Plans	Roll Back Procedures
Attack Surface Management	Snapshot Technologies

Vulnerability management is a proactive approach to identifying, classifying, remediating, and mitigating vulnerabilities in software and network systems. This process begins with the gathering of intelligence feeds, which provide up-to-date information on emerging threats and vulnerabilities from various sources, including vendors, industry consortia, and government agencies. These intel feeds are instrumental in helping organizations anticipate and respond to new vulnerabilities before they are exploited by attackers. To ensure that identified vulnerabilities accurately reflect the risks to the organization, a validation environment is essential. Such an environment mirrors the production environment, allowing for the safe testing of vulnerabilities and the assessment of potential impacts without risking the operational systems. Additionally, a well-structured communication plan is vital for vulnerability management. It ensures that stakeholders across the organization are informed about potential vulnerabilities, understand their roles in the mitigation process, and are aware of the progress towards resolution. Effective communication helps in coordinating responses to vulnerabilities and maintaining transparency with customers and partners regarding security efforts.

Attack surface management (ASM) is an essential component of comprehensive vulnerability management within enterprise security frameworks. It involves the systematic identification, classification, and monitoring of all possible entry points through which unauthorized users could potentially exploit a system. In the context of cybersecurity, the attack surface encompasses all the physical and digital aspects of an organization's environment that are accessible to and potentially exploitable by attackers. This includes network interfaces, software applications, web services, and even human elements like employees and contractors. By effectively managing the attack surface, organizations can proactively reduce their exposure to threats and vulnerabilities.

The first step in attack surface management is to identify and classify all assets within an organization's network, including servers, workstations, mobile devices, applications, and databases. This process not only involves mapping out what exists within the digital and physical environments but also understanding the potential vulnerabilities associated with each asset. Special attention is given to public-facing assets, such as web applications and external network interfaces, which are more susceptible to attacks.

Continuous monitoring of the identified assets is critical to detect changes in the attack surface. This includes tracking new devices being added to the network, software updates, changes in configurations, and the introduction of new services. Monitoring tools and techniques such as vulnerability scanners, intrusion detection systems (IDS), and security information and event management (SIEM) solutions play a crucial role in this phase. They help in analyzing the data collected to identify potential security gaps and vulnerabilities that could increase the attack surface.

With a comprehensive understanding of the organization's attack surface, security teams can then work on mitigating and reducing vulnerabilities. This often involves patching outdated software, removing unnecessary services or applications, enforcing stricter access controls, and segmenting networks to limit potential pathways for attackers. The principle of least privilege is applied rigorously to ensure that users and systems have only the access necessary to perform their functions, thereby minimizing the attack surface.

The dynamic nature of technology and business operations necessitates regular reviews and adjustments of the attack surface management strategy. As organizations adopt new technologies, launch new products, or change operational practices, the attack surface evolves. Periodic security assessments and penetration testing are essential to validate the effectiveness of current security measures and to identify new vulnerabilities.

Attack surface management is a proactive and continuous process that is integral to vulnerability management in enterprise security. By systematically identifying, monitoring, and mitigating potential entry points for attackers, organizations can significantly enhance their security posture. This not only helps in preventing security breaches but also ensures compliance with regulatory requirements and industry standards. Effective attack surface management requires a collaborative effort across different departments within an organization, leveraging technology, processes, and people to safeguard against evolving cybersecurity threats.

Patch management, an integral part of vulnerability management, involves the acquisition, testing, and installation of patches to fix vulnerabilities in software and systems. A critical component of successful patch management is the establishment of a testing environment that closely replicates the live production environment. This allows for the thorough testing of patches to verify that they do not introduce new vulnerabilities or negatively impact system functionality. Ensuring the use of realistic test data within this environment is crucial for accurately assessing the effects of patches on application performance and system behavior. Additionally, robust rollback procedures must be in place to quickly revert changes if a patch causes unforeseen issues, minimizing downtime and operational disruption. For organizations leveraging virtualization technologies, snapshot technologies offer a valuable tool in patch management strategies. They allow systems to be quickly restored to their pre-patch state, providing an additional safety net when deploying patches across critical systems.

Considerations for successful patch management		
Create System Inventory	Assign Risk Level	Reduce Variant/Versions
Updated announcement	Manage Expectations	Test before applying

Vulnerability (including attack surface management) and patch management are critical components of enterprise security, requiring careful planning, execution, and coordination. Through the integration of intel feeds, validation environments, and effective communication, organizations can proactively manage vulnerabilities. Meanwhile, patch management, supported by testing environments, realistic test data, rollback procedures, and snapshot technologies, ensures that vulnerabilities are promptly and safely remediated. Together, these practices form a comprehensive defense strategy that protects organizations from the ever-evolving landscape of cybersecurity threats, ensuring the resilience and reliability of their operational systems.

Availability Management

Availability management is a pivotal aspect of enterprise security, focusing on ensuring that critical systems and data remain accessible to users and operations even in the face of disruptions. This encompasses strategies and technologies aimed at maintaining high availability (HA) and effective disaster recovery (DR) planning, which are foundational to sustaining business continuity and resilience.

High Availability	Disaster Recovery
Load Balancers Stateless Design Reliable Messaging Redundancy of Components	Snapshots Log Replay 2 Phase Commits RTO/RPO

High Availability (HA) is designed to ensure that systems and applications are continuously operational, minimizing downtime and maintaining seamless access for users. HA strategies include the deployment of load balancers, which distribute incoming traffic across multiple servers to prevent any single point of failure from affecting the overall system availability. This is complemented by adopting a stateless design for applications, where sessions do not depend on a single server, enabling users to continue their activities uninterrupted even if one server goes down. Reliable messaging systems further enhance HA by ensuring that messages between components are delivered and processed reliably, even in the event of partial system failures. Redundancy is another critical element, where all components of the system, including servers, storage, and network paths, are duplicated to eliminate single points of failure. Such redundancy ensures that if one component fails, its backup can immediately take over, thus maintaining the system's availability.

Disaster Recovery (DR) focuses on the ability to recover from significant disruptions, such as natural disasters, cyberattacks, or system failures. DR planning revolves around key concepts such as snapshots and log replays, which facilitate the rapid restoration of data to a known good state. Snapshots capture the entire state of a system at specific points in time, allowing for quick restoration, while log replays can be used to recover more recent data changes up to the point of disruption. The two-phase commit protocol ensures transaction integrity across distributed systems, critical for maintaining consistent and reliable data after recovery. Central to DR planning are the Recovery Time Objective (RTO) and Recovery Point Objective (RPO). RTO defines the maximum acceptable time to restore operations after a disaster, while RPO sets the maximum age of files that must be recovered from backup storage for normal operations to resume without significant losses. These objectives guide the development of DR strategies, ensuring they align with business needs and risk tolerance levels.

In essence, availability management in enterprise security is about implementing proactive measures to prevent downtime (HA) and preparing responsive strategies to recover from it (DR). By embracing technologies like load balancers, stateless designs, reliable messaging, and redundancy, organizations can achieve high availability. Concurrently, through effective disaster recovery planning, leveraging snapshots, log replays, and understanding RTO and RPO, they ensure they can quickly bounce back from disruptions. Together, these strategies form a comprehensive approach to maintaining operational resilience, safeguarding against potential financial losses, reputational damage, and ensuring the continuous delivery of services essential for business success.

Supply Chain Security

Supply chain security in the context of enterprise cybersecurity is a concern that extends beyond the confines of a single organization to encompass the entire network of suppliers, partners, and customers involved in the production and distribution of goods and services. This holistic approach is necessary because vulnerabilities in any part of the supply chain can compromise the security of all entities within it. The interconnected nature of modern supply chains means that risks can quickly propagate upstream and downstream, highlighting the importance of securing every link in the chain.

Organizations must diligently assess and manage the cybersecurity risks associated with their upstream suppliers (those who provide products or services to the company) and downstream partners (those to whom the company provides products or services). Upstream dependencies are particularly concerning because a compromise at any supplier level can lead to infiltrations into an organization's systems, as seen in attacks where malicious actors use software updates or hardware components to breach network defenses. Downstream, organizations have a responsibility to ensure that their products and services do not expose customers and partners to cybersecurity vulnerabilities, necessitating stringent security measures throughout the development and distribution processes.

The use of open-source libraries in software development introduces a complex layer of supply chain risk, as vulnerabilities within these components can compromise the security of the broader application or system. This risk was starkly highlighted by the Heartbleed bug in

OpenSSL, a widely used open-source cryptographic library. Heartbleed exposed millions of websites to data leakage, demonstrating how a single flaw in a fundamental component could have far-reaching consequences for internet security. Similarly, the SolarWinds breach, though not rooted in an open-source library, underscored the dangers inherent in the software supply chain. Malicious code was inserted into SolarWinds' Orion software, used by thousands of companies and government agencies, enabling widespread espionage activities. These incidents underscore the critical need for rigorous security vetting and monitoring of both open-source and proprietary components within the software supply chain, to detect vulnerabilities early and mitigate potential risks effectively.

To mitigate risks associated with supply chain vulnerabilities, organizations should develop strategies for **alternative sourcing**. This involves identifying secondary suppliers for critical components or services that can be quickly engaged if a primary supplier is compromised or otherwise unable to fulfill its obligations. Alternative sourcing requires thorough vetting of potential suppliers' cybersecurity practices to ensure they meet the organization's security standards. This approach not only enhances resilience against cyber threats but also ensures business continuity in the face of supply chain disruptions.

Regular updates and upgrades are essential for maintaining the security of software and hardware components throughout the supply chain. Organizations should implement comprehensive update and upgrade plans that include mechanisms for securely distributing patches and updates to all elements of the supply chain. This includes ensuring that suppliers maintain robust security practices for the development and distribution of updates and that customers are promptly informed of necessary upgrades to maintain the security of products they have purchased. Effective update and upgrade plans also involve monitoring for new vulnerabilities and developing rapid response strategies to address them as soon as they are identified.

Supply chain security is a complex but essential aspect of enterprise cybersecurity. By carefully managing upstream and downstream dependencies, preparing alternative sourcing strategies, and implementing secure and efficient update and upgrade plans, organizations can significantly reduce their risk exposure and enhance the overall security of their supply chain. This not only protects the organization and its partners but also contributes to the integrity and resilience of the global digital ecosystem.

Security Operations Center (SOC)

Security Operations Center (SOC) technologies play another important role in the enterprise security architecture, offering the tools and platforms necessary to monitor, analyze, and respond to cybersecurity threats in real time. As the complexity of cyber threats continues to evolve, so too do the technologies employed by SOCs to defend against these threats. Among the core technologies foundational to SOC operations are Security Information and Event Management (SIEM), Security Orchestration, Automation, and Response (SOAR), and next-generation platforms like Microsoft Sentinel and Google Chronicle.

SIEM (Security Information and Event Management)

SIEM technology is central to SOC operations, providing a comprehensive view of an organization's information security. SIEM solutions collect, normalize, and aggregate log data from various sources across the enterprise, including network devices, systems, and applications. This data is then analyzed to identify patterns of behavior or anomalies that may indicate a security incident. SIEM platforms are designed to facilitate real-time visibility, event correlation, and alerting, enabling SOC analysts to quickly detect and investigate potential threats. They also support compliance reporting by maintaining historical data on security events.

SOAR (Security Orchestration, Automation, and Response)

SOAR platforms take the capabilities of SIEM one step further by adding layers of orchestration and automation to SOC operations. SOAR solutions enable organizations to standardize and automate response procedures, making it possible to handle a larger volume of alerts more efficiently. They orchestrate workflows across different security tools and automate repetitive tasks, freeing up analysts to focus on more complex investigations. SOAR tools also facilitate incident response by providing playbooks for common threat scenarios, ensuring consistent and swift action is taken to mitigate threats.

Next-Generation Platforms

Microsoft Sentinel: Microsoft Sentinel represents a leap forward in SOC technologies, being a cloud-native SIEM and SOAR solution that leverages the scalability and flexibility of the cloud. Sentinel integrates deeply with other Microsoft services and various third-party solutions, offering advanced analytics, artificial intelligence, and machine learning capabilities to enhance threat detection, investigation, and response. Its cloud-native nature allows for rapid deployment and scaling, making it accessible for organizations of all sizes.

Google Chronicle: Part of the Google Cloud Platform, Chronicle is designed to analyze and store massive amounts of security telemetry, leveraging Google's infrastructure and analytics capabilities. It focuses on speed and scalability, enabling security teams to process and analyze petabytes of data in real time. Chronicle's strength lies in its ability to leverage Google's vast threat intelligence and analytics capabilities, helping organizations identify threats more quickly and with greater accuracy than traditional systems.

Integration in Enterprise Security Architecture

The integration of SOC technologies like SIEM, SOAR, and next-generation platforms into the enterprise security architecture is crucial for maintaining situational awareness and responding effectively to cybersecurity threats. These technologies provide the backbone for monitoring security posture, detecting anomalies, automating response processes, and ensuring compliance with regulatory requirements. By leveraging advanced analytics, AI, and machine learning, next-generation platforms like Microsoft Sentinel and Google Chronicle offer enhanced capabilities for threat detection and response, marking a significant evolution in the tools available to SOCs.

SOC technologies are essential components of modern enterprise security architectures, enabling organizations to detect, analyze, and respond to cyber threats more efficiently and effectively. As cyber threats continue to evolve in complexity and volume, the role of advanced SOC technologies will become increasingly critical in safeguarding digital assets and ensuring the resilience of enterprise operations.

Mobile Device Security

Mobile device security is another growing area of enterprise security, reflecting the increasing reliance on smartphones and tablets within the corporate landscape. The proliferation of mobile devices introduces a complex array of security challenges that organizations must navigate to protect sensitive data and maintain operational integrity. These challenges are exacerbated by several factors, including the diversity of mobile operating systems (OS), the explosive growth of mobile applications, and the common practice of mixing business with personal devices.

There are many challenges in the management of Mobile Device Security. Firstly, there are a variety of mobile OS variants. The mobile ecosystem is fragmented, with numerous versions of Android and iOS in use at any given time. Newer Mobile OS like KaiOS and HarmonyOS are also on the rise. This diversity makes it difficult for organizations to ensure consistent security policies and protections across all employee devices. Each variant may have its own set of vulnerabilities, requiring distinct mitigation strategies. The vast number of applications available to users, coupled with the ease of installing them, increases the risk of introducing malicious software or leaky apps that could compromise corporate data or provide backdoors into secure environments.

The trend of Bring Your Own Device (BYOD) has blurred the lines between personal and business use, making it challenging to enforce security policies without infringing on personal privacy. This dual use increases the risk of data leakage, whether through lost devices, insecure apps, or phishing attacks targeted at less secure personal accounts.

Some of the potentially sensitive data that can be found on mobile devices include:

Call Detail Records (CDRs): Service providers frequently use CDRs to improve network performance. However, they can provide useful information to cyber criminals, as well. CDRs can show:

- Call started and ended date/time
- The terminating and originating towers
- Whether the call was outgoing or incoming
- Call time duration
- Who was called and who made the call

Global Positioning System (GPS): GPS data is an excellent source of empirical data. GPS can pinpoint a person's location as well as their actions. GPS also locates the movements of a person and it helps in finding phone call logs, images, and SMS messages.

App Data: Many apps store and access data the user is not aware of. In fact, many apps seek permission during the installation process to access these data. For example, photo or video editing apps request permission to access media files, camera, and GPS for navigation. This data can be a source of information to the cyber criminal.

SMS: Text messaging is a widely used way of communication. Text messages leave electronic records of dialogue that can be used by cyber criminals. They include the relevant information such as:

- Date/time of each message
- Phone number of sender and receiver

Photos and Videos: They can also be a tremendous source of information for cyber criminals to plan social engineering attacks.

To address these challenges, enterprises have turned to several key solutions designed to secure mobile devices and the data they access:

Mobile Device Management (MDM)

MDM solutions allow IT departments to remotely manage and secure mobile devices within their network. This includes enforcing security policies, pushing software updates, managing configurations, and remotely wiping data on lost or stolen devices. MDM solutions provide a centralized platform to ensure that all mobile devices comply with the organization's security standards, regardless of OS variations.

Mobile Application Management (MAM)

MAM focuses on controlling the internal and external applications installed on users' devices. This involves the distribution, updating, and securing of apps, with capabilities such as restricting access to app stores, whitelisting approved apps, and securing data within apps. MAM enables organizations to mitigate risks associated with the explosion of mobile apps by ensuring only approved, secure applications are used for business purposes.

Sandboxing

Sandboxing isolates applications or processes within a secure environment on the device, preventing them from interacting with core system functions or accessing data from other apps. This containment strategy is effective in minimizing the impact of a compromised app, protecting corporate data even if a device is used for both personal and business purposes.

Self-Destruction of Data

For highly sensitive information, some mobile security solutions offer self-destruction capabilities, where data is automatically deleted after a certain condition is met, such as a number of failed login attempts or if the device is reported lost or stolen. This ensures that sensitive data does not fall into the wrong hands, providing an ultimate line of defense against data breaches.

Mobile device security is a multifaceted challenge that requires a comprehensive approach to address. By implementing solutions like Mobile Device Management, Mobile Application Management, sandboxing, and self-destruction of data, organizations can navigate the complexities introduced by the diverse mobile landscape, the proliferation of apps, and the blending of personal and business device use. These strategies, combined with ongoing user education and a culture of security awareness, form the backbone of effective mobile device security in the enterprise context.

Cloud Security

In the evolving landscape of enterprise security architecture, the shift towards cloud computing has been one of the most transformative trends, reshaping how organizations approach data protection, application deployment, and infrastructure management. This chapter on cloud security aims to illuminate the nuanced security implications, challenges, and techniques inherent to cloud computing environments from the perspective of a security architect. Our objective is not to train cloud architects but to equip security professionals with a deep understanding of how cloud computing alters the security paradigm compared to traditional on-premises environments.

Central to the discussion of cloud security is the Shared Responsibility Model, a fundamental concept that delineates the security obligations of the cloud service provider (CSP) and the customer.

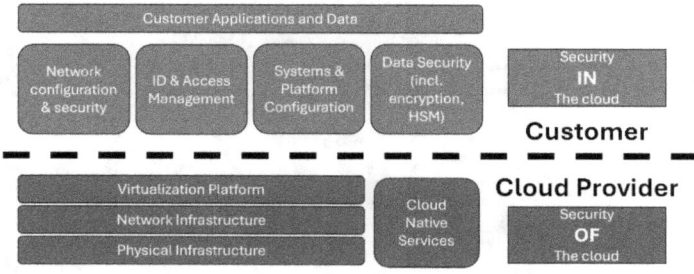

In traditional on-premises setups, the organization is solely responsible for securing all aspects of its IT infrastructure, from the physical security of data centers to the application layer's integrity. However, in cloud computing, this responsibility is divided. While the CSP takes charge of securing the cloud infrastructure itself, clients are responsible for protecting their data, applications, and access controls. This model necessitates a shift in how security architects conceptualize and implement security measures, underscoring the importance of understanding the specific responsibilities that fall to the organization within the cloud context.

Highlighting the key differences between traditional and cloud security, this chapter will delve into areas such as data sovereignty, identity and access management (IAM) in a distributed environment, and the complexities of data encryption in multi-tenant cloud architectures. We will explore how the elasticity and scalability of cloud services, while offering unprecedented flexibility and efficiency, also introduce new vulnerabilities and attack vectors that require innovative security approaches.

Moreover, we will address the unique challenges posed by different cloud service models—Infrastructure as a Service (IaaS), Platform as a Service (PaaS), and Software as a Service (SaaS)—each presenting distinct security considerations and requiring tailored strategies to ensure data integrity, confidentiality, and availability. The intricacies of securing cloud-native applications, the significance of automation in cloud security practices, and the critical role of compliance and governance in the cloud will also be examined. Below is a typical cloud security landscape.

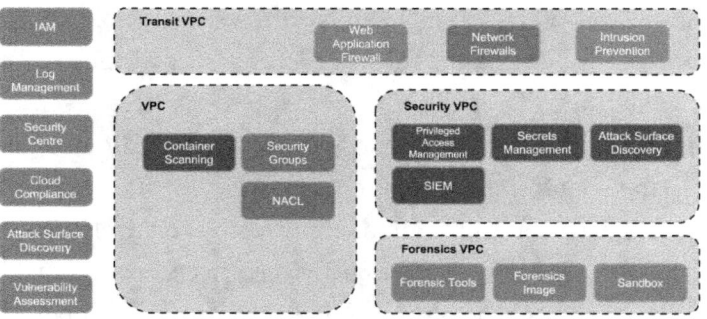

By the end of this chapter, security architects will have a comprehensive overview of the pivotal role cloud security plays in modern enterprise security architecture. Armed with this knowledge, they will be better prepared to navigate the complexities of cloud environments, implement robust security frameworks that leverage the cloud's strengths, and mitigate its potential risks. Embracing cloud security is not merely about adapting to a new technological domain; it's about reimagining security architectures in the context of the cloud's dynamic, distributed, and diverse nature.

Key Cloud Security Concepts

Understanding key concepts and the architectural framework is essential for security architects to effectively safeguard assets in the cloud. Here are a few key cloud security concepts that every security architect must keep in mind when working on the cloud.

Log Frequency and Timeliness

This pertains to the rate and regularity with which logs are recorded and how promptly they are made available for review. Different Cloud Service Providers (CSPs) offer various capabilities and services related to logging. Logs are a vital component of security for incident detection and response. They must be detailed and timely to enable quick action in the event of a security incident. Adjusting the log frequency and ensuring logs are produced without significant delay is crucial for maintaining a robust security posture in the cloud.

Privileged User Management

Privileged users have elevated access that can affect wide-ranging changes in the cloud environment, including the modification or deletion of critical resources. Managing these users effectively is vital to mitigate insider threats and reduce the risk of accidental or intentional misuse of cloud resources. Privileged user management involves implementing strict access controls, monitoring privileged sessions, and applying the principle of least privilege to minimize access to what is necessary for users to perform their job functions.

Secrets/Keys Management

In cloud environments, managing authentication secrets, such as API keys and passwords, is essential for securing access to applications and services. Secrets and keys must be protected with strong encryption, securely stored, and regularly rotated to prevent unauthorized access. CSPs often provide tools and services that help automate secrets management, enabling secure and efficient handling of these sensitive elements.

As a security architecture, do take note of these 3 key points which can differ from CSP to CSP.

Cloud Security Architecture Areas

Cloud Security Architecture is a multifaceted discipline that forms the backbone of cloud computing, ensuring that all aspects of a cloud environment are secure and resilient against potential cyber threats. Each area of the architecture plays a unique role in protecting the cloud ecosystem.

Cloud Infrastructure Scope

Cloud infrastructure comprises the virtualized resources that provide services over the internet in the cloud computing model. In terms of security, it is important to understand and implement the architectural features provided by cloud service providers (CSPs) to enhance resilience and reliability. Several key concepts—such as region, availability zones, multi-zone design, and service scope—are fundamental to cloud infrastructure and its security posture.

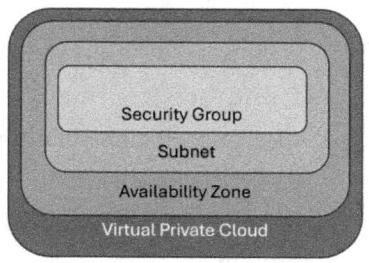

Region: A region in cloud infrastructure refers to a specific geographical area where a CSP operates data centers. These regions are typically chosen to reduce latency for regional end-users and to comply with local regulations regarding data sovereignty. From a security perspective, understanding regions is vital for disaster recovery planning and maintaining data residency as per compliance requirements. Organizations might choose to store sensitive data in regions that comply with specific legal or industry requirements regarding data storage and transfer.

Availability Zones: Within regions, CSPs often have multiple isolated locations known as Availability Zones (AZs). Each AZ is essentially a standalone data center with its own power, cooling, and networking resources to ensure fault tolerance and service continuity. Security-wise, the use of multiple AZs within the same region can protect against outages and localized disruptions. If one zone is compromised or experiences failure, the others can continue to operate, minimizing the risk of downtime.

Multi-Zone Design: A multi-zone design leverages multiple Availability Zones to increase the availability and fault tolerance of cloud services. In a multi-zone architecture, critical workloads are duplicated across different AZs, providing redundancy. This design principle is essential for ensuring continuous operation and is a key part of a robust disaster recovery strategy. From a security standpoint, it allows for graceful degradation of services in the event of an attack or failure, as traffic can be rerouted to unaffected zones without significant service impact.

Service Scope: Service scope pertains to the coverage and capabilities offered by a cloud service, including security features and responsibilities. Cloud services come in various models, such as Infrastructure as a Service (IaaS), Platform as a Service (PaaS), and Software as a Service (SaaS), each with different scopes of management and security responsibilities. Understanding the service scope is critical for security architects because it dictates which security controls are managed by the

CSP and which are the responsibility of the customer. The scope will influence how security measures such as firewall configurations, identity and access management, and application security need to be addressed.

cloud infrastructure security requires a comprehensive understanding of the architectural components and service scopes offered by cloud service providers. By utilizing concepts like regions, availability zones, and multi-zone designs, organizations can architect secure and resilient cloud environments. These elements, along with a clear grasp of the service scope, enable organizations to align their security strategies with the cloud model, ensuring that they leverage the full potential of cloud computing while maintaining a strong security posture.

Network Security

Cloud network security is an integral part of cloud architecture, focused on protecting the communications, applications, and data that traverse the virtualized networking infrastructure within cloud environments. The security of a cloud network is multi-layered and involves various components and services designed to ensure traffic isolation, protect data, and manage access to computing resources. Here's how different elements contribute to cloud network security:

Virtual Private Cloud (VPC)

A VPC is an isolated section within the cloud provider's network where you can launch resources in a virtual network that you define. It is the fundamental building block of cloud network security, providing a sandbox-like environment where organizations can control network configurations, including IP address ranges, subnets, route tables, and network gateways.

Subnets: Subnets allow for the partitioning of a VPC's IP address range into smaller segments, which can be used to isolate and manage groups of resources within a VPC. This aids in controlling access and reducing the potential for unauthorized network interactions.

Security Groups: These are virtual firewalls that provide stateful packet filtering for instances within a VPC. Security groups control inbound and outbound traffic to instances, ensuring that only allowed traffic as per the configured rules can flow to and from the compute resources.

Network Gateways

In the architecture of cloud networks, gateways serve as pivotal nodes that control data flow between different networks and environments. These specialized devices or services manage different aspects of network traffic, ensuring secure and efficient communication. Let's delve into four commonly used types of network gateways in cloud environments:

Internet Gateway: An internet gateway is a node that connects a company's internal network to the internet. In cloud environments, an internet gateway allows resources within a Virtual Private Cloud (VPC) to access and be accessed from the internet. It serves as a pathway for inbound and outbound traffic, acting as a mediator that translates internal private IP addresses to routable addresses for the wider internet. It's an essential component for any service within a VPC that needs to communicate with the internet, such as web servers or externally facing applications, and plays a key role in managing the security aspects of this communication by integrating with firewall rules and access policies.

NAT Gateway: A Network Address Translation (NAT) gateway enables instances in a private subnet within a VPC to initiate outbound traffic to the internet or other CSP services, while preventing inbound traffic from the internet. NAT gateways are typically used to enable private instances to download patches or updates while maintaining a secure and private environment that is not directly exposed to external threats. They are an important aspect of network security architecture, ensuring that only initiated connections can traverse in a controlled manner from the secure, private network to the public space.

API Gateway: An API gateway is a management tool that sits between a client and a collection of backend services. It acts as a reverse proxy to accept all application programming interface (API) calls, aggregate the various services required to fulfill them, and return the appropriate result. An API gateway provides a centralized point to enforce security and access control policies for APIs, enables throttling to manage traffic load, and can also handle API version management. From a security standpoint, API gateways can be configured to require authentication and authorization before allowing access to backend services, protecting against unauthorized use of APIs.

Virtual Private Gateway (VPG): This gateway connects on-premises networks to a VPC over a secure and private connection, often via a Virtual Private Network (VPN). A VPG serves as the VPC's side of this VPN connection. It can be an essential element for hybrid cloud architectures, allowing for the secure transmission of sensitive data between an organization's internal data center and the cloud environment. The VPG allows for encrypted connections, maintaining the confidentiality and integrity of data as it traverses potentially unsecured networks, such as the internet.

Each type of gateway serves a distinct function within the network architecture and provides various layers and controls for network traffic management and security. Internet gateways manage general traffic between the VPC and the internet, NAT gateways allow for secure outbound connections, API gateways manage and secure API traffic, and Virtual Private Gateways enable secure connections between different network environments. Proper configuration and management of these gateways are vital to maintaining a secure, efficient, and reliable cloud network infrastructure.

Load Balancers

Cloud load balancers are integral components of a robust security architecture within cloud environments. They play a role not only in distributing workloads to optimize resource utilization and prevent overloading systems but also in enhancing the security posture of cloud deployments.

Load balancers act as the traffic cops of a network, directing incoming network traffic across multiple servers or endpoints. This distribution process helps to ensure that no single server bears too much demand, which can improve the overall responsiveness and availability of applications. But beyond performance and scalability, load balancers contribute to security in several key ways:

Traffic Encryption: Load balancers can terminate SSL/TLS connections, offloading the encryption and decryption work from the application servers. This allows them to manage SSL certificates and encryption keys centrally, standardizing the secure handling of encrypted traffic and reducing the potential attack surface by limiting the exposure of private keys.

DDoS Mitigation: By balancing traffic across several resources, load balancers can absorb and disperse the high traffic volumes associated with Distributed Denial of Service (DDoS) attacks. Some advanced load balancers come with built-in DDoS mitigation tools that can detect and diffuse attack traffic to minimize impact on services.

Authentication and Authorization: Many load balancers offer integrated authentication and authorization capabilities, ensuring that only legitimate users and services are able to access backend resources. This can prevent unauthorized access and reduce the likelihood of attacks reaching the application layer.

Traffic Filtering: Load balancers can inspect incoming traffic and apply rules to filter out malicious requests, such as SQL injection or cross-site scripting attacks, before they reach the application servers. This makes them an essential part of defensive measures against application-layer attacks.

Redundancy and Failover: By distributing traffic across multiple servers, load balancers ensure that if one server fails, traffic is automatically rerouted to other healthy servers. This provides redundancy and ensures that services remain available even in the event of individual server failure.

Public and Internal Load Balancing: Cloud environments typically offer both public and internal load balancers. Public load balancers distribute traffic coming from the internet to your cloud environment, while internal load balancers distribute traffic within your cloud environment. This allows for segmentation of traffic and can help in maintaining different security levels for public-facing services and internal applications.

Isolation and Segmentation: Load balancers can also contribute to network segmentation strategies. By controlling which users or services can access certain resources, they can isolate sensitive applications and databases, reducing the risk of lateral movement within a network.

In essence, cloud load balancers play a multifaceted role in security architecture, beyond their primary function of traffic management. They help mitigate a range of threats and are vital in ensuring the availability, resilience, and security of cloud-based applications. For security architects, understanding and leveraging the capabilities of cloud load balancers is essential in designing defenses that are as dynamic and scalable as the cloud environments they protect.

Network Segmentation

Cloud network segmentation is a critical strategy in cloud security architecture, designed to limit the scope of access to resources within a cloud environment and reduce the potential impact of security breaches. By dividing larger networks into smaller, distinct segments, each with its own unique security policies and controls, organizations can contain and control the lateral movement of potential threats, effectively shrinking the attack surface that attackers can exploit. Some key aspects of cloud network segmentation includes:

Microsegmentation: This involves creating fine-grained security policies to control traffic between workloads at a granular level, often down to the individual workload or application. Microsegmentation is particularly useful in dynamic cloud environments, where workloads can frequently change and scale.

Subnetting: In cloud networks, subnets can be used to divide a larger network into logical segments at the IP layer. Subnets may represent different organizational units or service tiers, each with tailored security measures. This facilitates more precise control over inter-subnet traffic, enhancing security and simplifying policy enforcement.

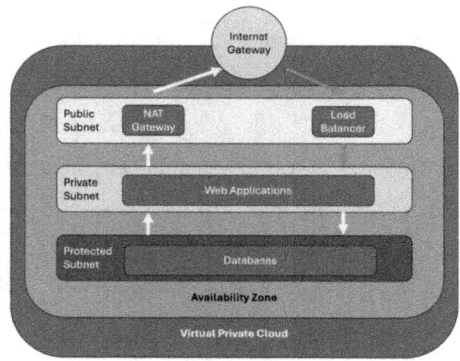

Virtual Network Peering: Secure connections between different cloud networks, or VPCs, enable segmentation across projects or even across different cloud providers. This helps to maintain network isolation while still allowing necessary inter-network communication. This will be covered in more details later.

Zero Trust Networks: The principle of "never trust, always verify" is baked into the network segmentation strategy. Each segment operates under the assumption that no user or system is trustworthy by default, regardless of their location within or outside of the network, thus enforcing strict access controls and authentication at every point.

Identity-Based Segmentation: Going beyond IP addresses, identity-based segmentation uses the identities of users or devices to determine access controls. This aligns with the shift towards identity as the new perimeter in cloud security, where access decisions are based on the identity of the requester rather than the network from which they originate.

Implementing cloud network segmentation effectively requires careful planning and ongoing management. It begins with a clear understanding of the data and resources that need protection, followed by designing the network topology to isolate these resources based on their sensitivity and the users' needs. As part of the security architecture, segmentation should be complemented with other security controls like monitoring, intrusion detection systems, and regular audits to ensure the segmentation rules are both effective and aligned with the organization's evolving security posture.

VPC Peering

VPC peering is a networking connection between two VPCs that enables you to route traffic between them using private IPv4 or IPv6 addresses. In the context of security architecture, VPC peering plays a crucial role by facilitating secure inter-VPC communications without the data traversing the public internet, thus maintaining a high level of security and reducing exposure to potential external threats. VPC peering contributes to security architecture in the following ways:

Isolation and Encapsulation: VPC peering allows different VPCs to communicate with each other as if they are on the same network while maintaining the boundary and isolation of each VPC. This isolation is key in preventing unauthorized access and minimizing the potential attack surface.

Controlled Access: With VPC peering, you can implement granular access controls using network access control lists (ACLs), security groups, and routing rules to regulate the traffic between peered VPCs. This precise control ensures that only authorized systems can interact, in line with the principle of least privilege.

Data Protection: Since the traffic between peered VPCs stays on the global infrastructure of the cloud provider, it benefits from the inherent security and privacy features of the cloud network. This reduces risks associated with data interception or eavesdropping that are more prevalent when data traverses the public internet.

Compliance and Data Residency: VPC peering can help in meeting compliance requirements related to data residency and sovereignty by ensuring that traffic between resources does not leave a particular geographic region, which could be a mandate for certain legal jurisdictions.

Network Performance and Reliability: Enhanced network performance and reliability indirectly contribute to security by reducing the chances of misconfiguration or performance-related disruptions that could make systems more vulnerable to attacks.

Scalability and Flexibility: As organizations grow and evolve, their network architecture must adapt. VPC peering allows for a scalable and flexible interconnection between VPCs that can grow as the organization's needs change, without compromising on security.

Reduced Complexity: VPC peering simplifies network architecture by reducing the need for complex routing, VPN connections, or other mechanisms that might be required for cross-VPC communication. Simplified architectures can often be more secure due to fewer components that could be misconfigured or exploited.

VPC peering is particularly relevant in scenarios where different projects, departments, or even organizations (such as partners or subsidiaries) must securely communicate within the cloud. It's crucial, however, for security architects to carefully design and manage these peer connections, as misconfigurations can lead to unintended data exposure.

Site-to-Site VPN

In cloud security architecture, a site-to-site VPN is an component that establishes a secure and encrypted connection between two distinct networks, such as an on-premises data center and a cloud provider's network, or between two cloud environments potentially across different geographical locations. This connection enables businesses to extend their data centers to the cloud securely and to leverage cloud resources as an extension of their existing network.

Site-to-Site VPNs function by encrypting the data originating from one site and decrypting it at the other site, thereby creating a "tunnel" through which data can travel securely over the internet. This encrypted tunnel prevents eavesdropping, tampering, and unauthorized access, ensuring that data remains confidential and integral as it traverses untrusted public networks.

Site-to-site VPNs are vital for securing data communication in a cloud environment. They allow organizations to extend their networks into the cloud securely, ensuring that sensitive information is protected during transit over the internet. As part of cloud security architecture, site-to-site VPNs must be properly configured, managed, and integrated with other security measures to protect against cybersecurity threats while enabling seamless connectivity between disparate network environments.

VPC Endpoints

VPC endpoints are a cloud networking component that allows private connections between a Virtual Private Cloud (VPC) and other services offered by the cloud provider without requiring the traffic to pass over the internet. In the context of security architecture, VPC endpoints enhance the security posture by enabling secure and private communications to services that would otherwise be accessed over the public internet. Cloud providers typically offer two types of VPC endpoints: interface endpoints (powered by AWS PrivateLink, for example) that allow connectivity to a variety of services, and gateway endpoints that are specific to certain services (like Amazon S3 and DynamoDB in AWS). The service-specific nature of these endpoints helps in applying narrowly scoped security controls tailored to the particular characteristics and requirements of each service.

VPC endpoints are a vital feature within cloud security architectures, providing secure, private connectivity to cloud services, which helps in maintaining data confidentiality and integrity. Their ability to support fine-grained access control policies and integration with IAM makes them an essential tool for enforcing network security policies. By enabling direct access to cloud services without traversing the internet, VPC endpoints significantly reduce the exposure to external threats and are thus an important consideration for any organization looking to secure their cloud-based resources.

Network Security Services

Cloud network security services are components of cloud security, providing the tools and mechanisms necessary to protect data, applications, and infrastructure within cloud environments. Among these services, Security Groups and Network Access Control Lists (NACLs) play pivotal roles in defining and enforcing access controls to secure cloud resources. Both services offer complementary capabilities for filtering traffic at different levels of the network architecture.

Security Groups act as virtual firewalls for instances (such as virtual machines) within a cloud environment. They are used to control inbound and outbound traffic at the instance level, offering stateful filtering capabilities. This means that any changes applied to incoming traffic rules are automatically reflected in the outbound rules, allowing for dynamic adjustments to traffic permissions based on the context of established connections. Key features of security groups include:

Stateful Inspection: Security Groups track the state of network connections (TCP/UDP streams) and automatically allow response traffic to inbound requests without requiring explicit outbound rules.

Instance-Level Filtering: They apply to instances within the Virtual Private Cloud (VPC), enabling granular control over the types of traffic that can reach each instance.

Default Deny: Security Groups typically default to denying all inbound traffic, requiring explicit rules to allow specific traffic types, thereby enforcing a principle of least privilege.

Easy to Modify: Rules within a Security Group can be easily modified, allowing for flexible and rapid adjustments to the security posture as needed.

Network Access Control Lists (NACLs) provide a layer of security at the subnet level within a VPC, offering stateless filtering of inbound and outbound traffic. Unlike Security Groups, NACLs do not track the state of network connections, requiring separate inbound and outbound rules to manage the flow of traffic in both directions. Key features of NACLs include:

Subnet-Level Filtering: NACLs apply to all the instances within a subnet, providing a broad layer of security that complements the more granular controls offered by Security Groups.

Stateless Filtering: Each packet is evaluated independently, without consideration for the connection's state, necessitating explicit rules for allowed inbound and outbound traffic.

Rule Evaluation Order: NACLs evaluate rules in numerical order, starting with the lowest number rule. This allows for the organization of rules by priority, with explicit "allow" and "deny" actions.

Separate Inbound and Outbound Rules: Administrators must configure separate rules for inbound and outbound traffic, giving them precise control over the flow of data into and out of a subnet.

Together, Security Groups and NACLs provide a robust framework for securing cloud networks. Security Groups offer the flexibility and precision needed for instance-level traffic filtering, ideal for managing access to specific cloud resources. In contrast, NACLs provide an additional layer of defense at the subnet level, allowing for broader control over traffic entering and leaving network segments. By carefully configuring these services, security architects can create a layered defense strategy that significantly reduces the attack surface of cloud environments, safeguarding against unauthorized access and potential threats.

Compute Security

Compute security in the cloud encompasses a broad range of technologies and approaches designed to protect data, applications, and services that run on cloud-based computational resources. This includes securing traditional virtual machines (VMs), modern containerized applications, serverless computing models, and understanding the nuances of cloud tenancy. Additionally, as organizations increasingly adopt microservices architectures, securing these distributed systems becomes critical.

Virtual Machines (VMs)

Virtual machines are emulations of physical computers that run an operating system and applications as if they were on a physical machine. Security for VMs includes ensuring the integrity of the hypervisor, the software, firmware, or hardware that creates and runs VMs. It also involves securing the VMs themselves through traditional security measures such as antivirus software, firewalls, and intrusion detection systems. Patch management and configuration management are vital to keep both the hypervisor and the VMs secure against known vulnerabilities.

Containers and Kubernetes Security

Containers provide a lightweight, portable, and consistent environment for applications to run in isolation from other processes. Kubernetes, an orchestration system for containers, automates the deployment, scaling, and management of containerized applications. Security for containers and Kubernetes involves securing the container runtime environment, the containers themselves, and the orchestration layer. This includes ensuring container images are free from vulnerabilities, implementing network policies to control the flow of traffic between containers, and securing the Kubernetes control plane and worker nodes against unauthorized access.

Serverless Computing Security

Serverless computing allows developers to build and run applications without managing servers. Security in a serverless architecture focuses on securing the application code and managing permissions and access to cloud services that the serverless functions interact with. Since the cloud provider manages the underlying infrastructure, the attack surface is different compared to traditional or containerized applications. Emphasis is placed on application-level security measures such as input validation, dependency management, and identity and access management (IAM) configurations.

Cloud Tenancy

Cloud tenancy refers to the architecture of cloud computing resources in terms of their physical and virtual separation.

Shared Tenancy: In a shared tenancy model, multiple customers' workloads run on the same physical hardware, isolated at the virtualization layer. This model offers cost savings but can raise concerns about "noisy neighbors" and potential for cross-tenant attacks.

Dedicated Instance: A dedicated instance runs on hardware that's exclusively used by a single customer but may share physical hosts with other instances from the same customer. This offers a middle ground between shared tenancy and fully dedicated hardware.

Dedicated Host: A dedicated host is a physical server fully dedicated to a single customer's use. This model provides the highest level of isolation and control, useful for compliance with strict regulatory requirements or for workloads that require specific server configurations.

Microservice Security

Microservices architectures involve developing applications as a collection of small, loosely coupled services. Security in a microservices architecture requires a shift in approach, focusing on securing the communication between services, implementing robust authentication and authorization for service-to-service interactions, and ensuring each microservice is individually secured against attacks. Techniques such as service meshes can provide transparent encryption, traffic control, and observability to enhance security without burdening individual microservices with these responsibilities.

Compute security in the cloud is a multifaceted domain requiring comprehensive strategies that address the specific characteristics and vulnerabilities of VMs, containers, serverless functions, and microservices. Understanding the implications of cloud tenancy options is also crucial for making informed decisions about workload deployment to meet security, performance, and compliance requirements. Each compute model and tenancy option presents unique challenges and opportunities for securing cloud-based applications and data, demanding a tailored approach to ensure robust protection across all layers of the cloud stack.

Storage Security

Protecting data at rest in the cloud is crucial. Cloud storage security encompasses encryption practices, access controls, and data lifecycle management to ensure that only authorized users can access cloud storage resources, and data is handled securely throughout its existence. Cloud storage comes in various forms, each with unique security considerations and mechanisms. The primary types of cloud storage include virtual disks, object storage, file storage, and databases. Let's explore the security aspects of each.

Virtual Disk

Virtual disks in the cloud act similarly to physical disks but are stored on virtualized storage infrastructure. They are often used by virtual machines and can be encrypted to protect data at rest. Encryption is the cornerstone of virtual disk security, with keys managed by the cloud provider or the customer using a key management service. Additionally, access controls and network security policies can restrict who can attach or detach these disks from instances, preventing unauthorized data access.

Object Storage

Object storage, designed for scalability and accessibility, requires robust data encryption, both at rest and during transmission, to safeguard against unauthorized access and eavesdropping. The implementation of detailed access policies provides granular control over who can interact with stored objects, further enhancing the security posture of object storage solutions.

File Storage

File storage in the cloud mimics traditional file systems and is optimized for shared access scenarios, necessitating network isolation techniques and user-level permissions to secure data. Mechanisms such as regular snapshots and backups are essential for recovering from data loss incidents, including accidental deletions and ransomware attacks. Additionally, file storage can be configured to allow access only from specific network segments or VPN connections to minimize exposure to potential attackers. Like traditional file systems, cloud file storage systems allow for the setting of user and group-level permissions to control access to files and directories. Regular snapshots and backups can protect against data loss due to accidental deletion or ransomware attacks, with the ability to restore to previous states.

Databases

Cloud databases, offering managed database services, emphasize the importance of encryption for data at rest and in transit, coupled with strong access management protocols to regulate database access. Monitoring database activity is crucial for identifying and mitigating unauthorized or anomalous access patterns, ensuring the database's security.

General Security Considerations for Cloud Storage

Across these cloud storage types, general security principles such as data lifecycle management play a vital role in dictating the retention and secure deletion of data, aligning with compliance mandates and minimizing data exposure risks. Assessing the security practices of cloud storage providers, including their adherence to industry standards and the robustness of their data center security measures, is essential for selecting a provider that matches an organization's security and compliance requirements.

Securing cloud storage requires a comprehensive approach tailored to the specific types of storage being used and the sensitivity of the data stored. By applying robust encryption, access controls, network security measures, and compliance practices, organizations can significantly enhance the security of their cloud storage environments, protecting against unauthorized access and data breaches.

Secrets Management

Cloud secrets management is another component of cloud security architecture, addressing the need to securely store, access, and manage sensitive information such as API keys, credentials, and cryptographic keys. As enterprises move more of their operations to the cloud, the importance of implementing robust secrets management practices becomes paramount to prevent data breaches and unauthorized access.

Types of Key Management

In the public cloud domain, there are various types of key management practices.

Hardware Security Modules (HSMs) are physical devices designed to safeguard and manage digital keys. In a cloud environment, cloud providers offer HSMs as a service, allowing organizations to benefit from high security for key management without managing physical hardware. HSMs provide strong isolation for keys, performing cryptographic operations within a tamper-resistant hardware environment.

Cloud Key Management Services (KMS) is a managed service that enables customers to create, manage, and use cryptographic keys for various services securely. These keys can be used to encrypt data at rest or in transit. Cloud KMS solutions often integrate with other cloud services, providing a seamless way to apply encryption and decryption operations across the cloud environment.

Beyond key management, **secrets managers** are dedicated tools for handling a broader range of secrets, including passwords, tokens, and certificates. These services not only store secrets securely but also provide controlled access based on policies, audit logs for tracking secret usage, and interfaces for applications to retrieve secrets dynamically.

Key Rotation Practices

Key rotation refers to the practice of regularly changing encryption keys and secrets to reduce the risk of key compromise. Effective key rotation practices are vital for maintaining the confidentiality and integrity of encrypted data over time.

Many secrets management and key management services offer **automated rotation** features, where keys and secrets are automatically changed at predefined intervals. This ensures that keys are regularly updated without manual intervention, reducing the operational overhead and minimizing the risk of oversight.

When rotating keys or secrets, it's important to implement versioning, where new keys are introduced and old keys are phased out gradually. This approach allows applications and services to transition smoothly to using the new keys without disrupting operations. Versioning also ensures that data encrypted with older keys remains accessible for a period, facilitating decryption operations even after new keys are in use.

Key rotation practices should adhere to the **principle of least privilege**, ensuring that only entities that need access to the keys for their operational role have such access. This minimizes the risk of unauthorized access during the rotation process.

Effective rotation practices are complemented by comprehensive auditing and monitoring to track key usage, access patterns, and potential security incidents. This visibility is crucial for identifying unauthorized access attempts or misuse of keys and secrets.

Incorporating cloud secrets management into the security architecture is essential for protecting sensitive data and ensuring secure operations in the cloud. By leveraging HSMs, cloud KMS, secrets managers, and adhering to best practices in key rotation, organizations can significantly enhance their security posture. These practices not only safeguard cryptographic keys and secrets but also contribute to a resilient and trustworthy cloud environment.

Cloud Identity and Access Management

Cloud IAM is a foundational component of enterprise security architecture, particularly as organizations increasingly adopt cloud-based services. Cloud IAM provides the framework and mechanisms for ensuring that the right individuals have access to the appropriate resources within the cloud environment, and that this access is securely managed and controlled at all times. It addresses the challenges of identity verification, access rights management, and the enforcement of security policies across a distributed cloud infrastructure.

Centralized Identity Management

Cloud IAM enables centralized management of user identities, integrating across cloud services and applications. This centralization simplifies the administration of user accounts and access rights, allowing security teams to maintain oversight over who has access to what resources. It supports single sign-on (SSO) capabilities, reducing password fatigue among users and minimizing the risk of credential compromise.

Granular Access Control

Granular access control is a core feature of cloud IAM, enabling detailed specification of access rights based on user roles, responsibilities, and the principle of least privilege. This means users are granted only the access necessary to perform their job functions, limiting the potential for unauthorized access or data breaches. Access controls can be applied to various cloud resources, including compute instances, storage buckets, and network configurations.

Multi-Factor Authentication (MFA)

Cloud IAM systems often incorporate multi-factor authentication (MFA) to enhance security by requiring two or more forms of verification before granting access. MFA adds an additional layer of protection beyond just passwords, such as a code from a smartphone app or a fingerprint scan, making it much harder for attackers to gain unauthorized access.

Identity Federation and Single Sign-On (SSO)

Identity federation allows users to securely access multiple cloud services and applications using a single set of credentials. This is achieved through standards such as SAML (Security Assertion Markup Language) and OAuth, facilitating seamless SSO experiences across cloud and on-premises environments. Federation and SSO simplify the user experience while maintaining strong security controls over access.

Auditing and Compliance Reporting

Cloud IAM solutions provide comprehensive tools for auditing and compliance reporting, enabling organizations to track access patterns, changes in permissions, and other security-relevant events. This capability is crucial for detecting potential security incidents and demonstrating compliance with regulatory requirements, such as GDPR, HIPAA, and SOC 2.

Automated Provisioning and De-provisioning

Automating the provisioning and de-provisioning of access rights is another important aspect of cloud IAM. This ensures that users receive prompt access to necessary resources upon joining an organization or changing roles and that access is revoked when it is no longer needed or when a user leaves the organization. Automation reduces the risk of human error and ensures timely management of access rights.

In the context of enterprise security architecture, cloud IAM plays a pivotal role in protecting cloud environments from unauthorized access and potential security breaches. By providing robust tools for managing identities, enforcing access controls, and monitoring and reporting on access-related activities, cloud IAM systems enable organizations to secure their cloud deployments effectively. As cloud computing continues to evolve, the role of cloud IAM in ensuring the security and compliance of cloud resources will only grow in importance.

Cloud Logging and Monitoring

Cloud Logging and Monitoring are indispensable components of a comprehensive security architecture in cloud environments. These practices involve the collection, analysis, and management of logs and metrics to detect, respond to, and prevent security incidents. Effective logging and monitoring strategies enhance visibility into cloud operations, enabling organizations to keep a pulse on the security health of their cloud infrastructure.

Security logging in the cloud entails the systematic collection and storage of logs from various cloud resources and services. These logs provide detailed records of events, transactions, and activities that occur within the cloud environment. By analyzing these logs, security teams can identify patterns of normal behavior and detect deviations that may indicate a security threat or vulnerability. Logs are crucial for forensic analysis, helping to trace the steps of an attacker, understand the scope of a breach, and identify the affected resources.

Monitoring extends beyond logging to include real-time analysis and alerting based on the data collected from cloud environments. This can involve monitoring for suspicious activities, such as unusual API calls or unexpected changes in configurations, which could signify an attempted breach or misconfiguration. Security monitoring tools can automatically alert security personnel to potential threats, enabling rapid response to mitigate risks. Moreover, monitoring is essential for compliance with industry standards and regulations, which often require continuous oversight of cloud environments to ensure data protection and privacy.

Key Components and Practices

Centralized Log Management: Aggregating logs from all cloud services and applications into a centralized log management solution is critical for effective analysis. Centralization enables correlation of events across different sources, providing a holistic view of the security posture.

Automated Alerting Systems: Configuring automated alerts based on predefined criteria or anomaly detection helps ensure that potential security issues are promptly addressed. These systems can trigger notifications or automated response actions based on the severity of detected events.

Integration with SIEM Tools: Integrating cloud logging and monitoring with Security Information and Event Management (SIEM) tools allows for advanced analytics, correlation, and reporting. SIEM tools can analyze log data in the context of broader security intelligence, enhancing the detection of sophisticated threats.

Continuous Compliance Monitoring: Regularly scanning cloud environments against compliance frameworks and best practices ensures that configurations adhere to security policies and regulatory requirements. This continuous monitoring supports compliance efforts and identifies gaps that need remediation.

Audit Trails for Forensic Analysis: Maintaining comprehensive and immutable logs supports forensic analysis in the aftermath of a security incident. Audit trails can provide a detailed record of actions taken by users and systems, crucial for investigating breaches and implementing improvements.

Anomaly Detection and Behavioral Analytics: Leveraging machine learning and behavioral analytics to detect anomalies in log and monitoring data can uncover complex threats that evade traditional detection methods. These technologies can identify unusual patterns that may indicate compromised accounts or insider threats.

In the world of cloud computing, Security Logging and Monitoring are foundational to maintaining a robust security architecture. These practices equip organizations with the necessary tools and insights to proactively manage security risks, ensuring the integrity, confidentiality, and availability of cloud-based resources. As cloud environments become more complex, the role of logging and monitoring in identifying and responding to security challenges becomes increasingly critical, underscoring the need for continuous innovation and investment in these areas.

Compliance and Security Best Practices

In the cloud computing landscape, ensuring compliance and adhering to security best practices are essential for protecting data, maintaining privacy, and upholding trust. Cloud compliance and security best practices form the bedrock of a robust cloud security architecture, guiding organizations in implementing effective controls and procedures to mitigate risks, adhere to regulatory standards, and foster a culture of security.

Compliance in the Cloud

Compliance in the cloud involves conforming to laws, regulations, and standards that govern data protection and privacy. This can include:

Regulatory Compliance: Adhering to regulations such as GDPR for data protection, HIPAA for healthcare information, and PCI DSS for payment data.

Industry Standards: Following best practices and standards set by frameworks such as ISO 27001 for information security management, NIST for cybersecurity, and SOC 2 for service organization controls.

Compliance requires a thorough understanding of the specific obligations relevant to an organization's industry and operational geography. Cloud providers often offer compliance programs and certifications to help customers navigate these requirements, but ultimate responsibility lies with the organization to ensure their cloud deployments meet all regulatory and standard requirements.

Security Best Practices

To end this chapter, we would reinforce the points made in the earlier sections as adopting security best practices is crucial for safeguarding assets in the cloud. These practices provide guidelines for setting up a secure cloud environment, encompassing various aspects of cloud security.

Data Encryption: Encrypting data at rest and in transit to protect sensitive information from unauthorized access. Utilization of built-in encryption services offered by cloud providers simplifies this process.

Access Management: Implementing strong access controls and identity management practices, including the principle of least privilege, to ensure only authorized users can access cloud resources. This includes using multi-factor authentication (MFA) and managing permissions with roles and policies.

Secure Configuration: Hardening cloud environments by configuring services securely by default, turning off unnecessary features, and regularly reviewing configurations to prevent misconfigurations that could lead to vulnerabilities.

Monitoring and Logging: Continuously monitoring cloud environments for unusual activities and maintaining logs for audit trails. Cloud providers offer tools for real-time monitoring and alerting, which can be integrated with incident response plans.

Patch Management: Regularly updating and patching cloud services and applications to protect against known vulnerabilities. Automated patch management services can help in maintaining the currency of systems.

Data Backup and Disaster Recovery: Implementing robust data backup and disaster recovery plans to ensure business continuity. Cloud environments offer scalable solutions for backups and replicas across regions, enhancing resilience against data loss and outages.

Network Security: Securing network access to cloud resources using firewalls, virtual private networks (VPNs), and network segmentation techniques. This includes minimizing exposure to the public internet and controlling inter-service communication within the cloud.

Continuous Compliance and Security Improvement

Maintaining compliance and security in the cloud is not a one-time effort but a continuous process. Organizations should regularly assess their cloud environments against compliance requirements and evolving security threats. This involves conducting regular security assessments, penetration testing, and compliance audits to identify and address gaps.

Furthermore, fostering a culture of security awareness among employees and stakeholders is critical. Training programs and regular communication about security policies and threats can empower individuals to act securely and responsibly in the cloud.

In summary, cloud compliance and security best practices are integral to establishing a secure foundation for cloud deployments. By diligently adhering to regulatory requirements, implementing best practices, and fostering an ongoing commitment to security and compliance, organizations can navigate the complexities of cloud security and harness the full potential of cloud computing while protecting their assets and maintaining trust with customers.

Each of the above areas requires a coordinated approach and the integration of various tools, policies, and practices to ensure the cloud environment is secure. As enterprises continue to move critical workloads to the cloud, a robust cloud security architecture becomes indispensable for managing the complexities of cloud security and ensuring the confidentiality, integrity, and availability of data in the cloud.

By covering these areas and concepts, security architects can craft comprehensive strategies that address the multifaceted nature of cloud security challenges. It is important to integrate these considerations seamlessly into the security architecture to protect against both internal and external threats effectively.

Cybersecurity Processes

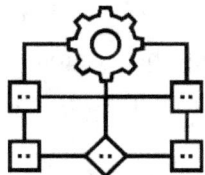

In enterprise security architecture, cybersecurity processes stand as the orchestrator of a robust defense strategy against the myriad of threats facing modern organizations. These processes encompass a comprehensive approach to identifying, managing, and mitigating risks, ensuring compliance with regulatory standards, and responding effectively to security incidents. At the core of this approach are three fundamental areas: risk management, audit and compliance, and incident response.

Risk Management is the foundational element that informs the security posture of an organization. It involves the systematic identification, assessment, and prioritization of risks to the organization's information assets and technologies. Effective risk management is a continuous process, requiring regular reviews to adapt to the ever-changing threat landscape. It enables organizations to allocate resources efficiently, focusing on areas of highest risk and implementing controls that balance the need for security with business objectives.

Audit and Compliance serve as the mechanisms through which organizations ensure adherence to internal policies and external regulatory requirements. This area encompasses the evaluation of security controls, policies, and procedures against established standards and frameworks such as ISO 27001, GDPR, HIPAA, and SOC 2. Through regular audits, organizations can identify gaps in their security architecture, providing a roadmap for enhancements and demonstrating compliance to regulators, partners, and customers. Compliance not only minimizes legal and financial risks but also reinforces an organization's commitment to protecting sensitive data and maintaining customer trust.

Incident Response is the organized approach to addressing and managing the aftermath of a security breach or attack. The goal is to handle the situation in a way that limits damage, reduces recovery time and costs, and mitigates any negative impact on the organization. An effective incident response plan entails preparation, detection and analysis, containment, eradication, and recovery, followed by a post-incident review to refine the response strategy. This process relies on strong coordination among IT, security, legal, and communications teams to manage the incident efficiently and communicate with stakeholders transparently.

Cybersecurity processes are integral to the enterprise security architecture, providing a structured framework for managing the complex interplay between technology, people, and policies. By emphasizing proactive risk management, diligent audit and compliance, and swift incident response, organizations can build a resilient security posture that not only protects against current threats but also anticipates and prepares for future challenges.

Risk Management

Risk management is another important pillar of cybersecurity architecture, providing a strategic framework to identify, assess, manage, and monitor the risks associated with an organization's information assets and technologies.

Risk Categories

Risks can be broadly categorized into three types: administrative, technical, and physical. Each type requires a tailored approach to management and mitigation.

Administrative Risks

These are related to the policies, procedures, and operations within an organization. They can include inadequate security policies, lack of employee training, or ineffective governance practices. To manage administrative risks, organizations should implement comprehensive security policies, conduct regular staff training on security awareness, perform background checks, and establish clear procedures for responding to security incidents.

Technical Risks

These involve risks associated with technology infrastructure, such as outdated systems, software vulnerabilities, or insufficient network security controls. Managing technical risks typically involves regular system and application updates, patch management, secure coding practices, and the deployment of security technologies like firewalls, antivirus programs, and intrusion detection systems.

Physical Risks

These are the risks to physical assets, like data centers, servers, and workstations. Physical risks can range from natural disasters damaging hardware to unauthorized access to sensitive areas. Protective measures include physical access controls, surveillance systems, environmental controls, and disaster recovery planning.

Risk Treatment

Risk treatment, or the process of dealing with identified risks, can be classified into four classes: preventive, detective, corrective, and compensating.

Preventive Measures

These are designed to prevent security incidents before they occur. Examples include access controls to prevent unauthorized entry, encryption to prevent data breaches, and network segmentation to prevent lateral movement by attackers.

Detective Measures

These are implemented to identify and signal the occurrence of a security event promptly. Detective measures include intrusion detection systems, security event log monitoring, and regular system audits.

Corrective Measures

These are actions taken to rectify the impact of a security incident after it has occurred. Corrective measures include patching affected systems, isolating compromised areas of the network, and restoring systems from backups.

Compensating Measures

These are alternative controls used to achieve the same objective as the original control when it is not feasible to implement the primary measure. Compensating measures may include additional monitoring, increased auditing, or manual processes to mitigate risk.

Lastly, it's essential to consider residual risk, which is the level of risk remaining after controls have been applied. Not all risks can be completely eliminated, and residual risk must be accepted, monitored, and reviewed regularly to ensure it remains within acceptable levels as determined by the organization's risk appetite. The residual risk must be communicated to stakeholders and factored into the organization's overall security strategy.

Effective risk management in cybersecurity architecture is a dynamic and continuous process that requires regular review and adaptation to new threats, vulnerabilities, and business processes. Effective risk management is critical for making informed decisions about securing assets while supporting business objectives. It encompasses several key components: risk assessment, risk analysis, risk mitigation, risk monitoring, and managing residual risk.

Risk Assessment

Risk assessment is the process of identifying and cataloging the cybersecurity risks that an organization faces. This involves enumerating assets, identifying potential threats to those assets, and determining the vulnerabilities that could be exploited by the threats. The goal is to create a comprehensive inventory of risks based on the likelihood of occurrence and potential impact on the organization. This step sets the foundation for all subsequent risk management activities by highlighting areas of concern that need attention.

Risk Analysis

Risk analysis dives deeper into the risks identified during the assessment phase to evaluate their potential impact on the organization. This analysis considers both qualitative and quantitative factors to prioritize risks according to their severity. Quantitative analysis may involve calculating potential financial losses, while qualitative analysis assesses the impact on reputation, operational efficiency, or compliance. The outcome of risk analysis guides organizations in allocating resources effectively to address the most significant risks.

Risk Mitigation

Risk mitigation involves implementing controls and strategies to reduce the likelihood or impact of identified risks. This can include deploying new security technologies, enhancing policies and procedures, training employees, or making architectural changes to systems. Risk mitigation strategies are selected based on their cost-effectiveness and their ability to reduce risk to an acceptable level. It's a balancing act between securing the organization and enabling it to achieve its business goals without undue restriction.

Risk Monitoring

Risk monitoring is the continuous observation of the organization's risk environment to detect changes in risk levels. This process includes tracking the effectiveness of implemented controls, identifying new risks as the organization evolves, and adjusting risk mitigation strategies in response to new threats or vulnerabilities. Effective risk monitoring ensures that the organization remains responsive to the dynamic cybersecurity landscape.

Residual Risk

Residual risk refers to the level of risk that remains after controls have been implemented. No risk mitigation measures are entirely foolproof, and there will always be some level of risk that cannot be eliminated. Managing residual risk involves accepting, transferring, avoiding, or further mitigating these risks, depending on their potential impact on the organization. It requires a strategic decision by management, often based on risk tolerance levels and the cost-benefit analysis of additional mitigation efforts. Below is a simple flow to determine residual risk.

In the broader context of cybersecurity architecture, risk management is an iterative and ongoing process. It provides a structured approach to managing cybersecurity risks in a way that supports strategic business objectives. By comprehensively covering risk assessment, analysis, mitigation, monitoring, and the management of residual risk, organizations can create a resilient cybersecurity posture that protects critical assets while navigating the complexities of the digital world.

Audit and Compliance

In the structured realm of enterprise security architecture, audit and compliance form the evaluative backbone that ensures not just the soundness of security practices, but also their alignment with regulatory and industry standards. This section delves into the world of audit and compliance, navigating through the nuances of periodic versus ad-hoc audits, the utility of reporting dashboards, the rigor of compliance remediation, and the emerging paradigm of compliance as code.

Periodic audits are systematic examinations scheduled at regular intervals. These audits provide a consistent framework for evaluating an organization's adherence to security policies, procedures, and controls. They are instrumental in establishing a rhythm of accountability and continuous improvement within an enterprise's security posture. On the other hand, ad-hoc audits are triggered by specific events or identified risks and are designed to target particular aspects of the security architecture. These can be incredibly valuable in the wake of security incidents or significant changes within the IT environment, offering a deep-dive into problem areas or emerging threats.

Reporting dashboards play a pivotal role in audit and compliance, translating the intricate data collected during audits into actionable intelligence. These dashboards offer real-time visibility into an organization's security status, providing key metrics, trends, and insights that empower decision-makers. They also serve as a critical communication tool, presenting complex compliance information in an accessible manner to stakeholders across the organization.

Compliance remediation involves the actions taken in response to audit findings. It is a critical step in addressing vulnerabilities and gaps in the security framework. Remediation efforts may range from simple fixes to complex system overhauls, each aimed at ensuring the organization meets its compliance obligations and mitigates potential security risks.

"Compliance as Code" represents the innovative intersection of IT and compliance disciplines. In this approach, compliance specifications are translated into code, enabling automated and continuous enforcement of compliance policies. This transformative concept aligns with the DevSecOps movement, embedding compliance checks directly into the development and deployment pipelines, thus streamlining the audit process and ensuring that compliance is an integral part of the system lifecycle from the outset.

In the broader context of enterprise security architecture, audit and compliance are not merely checkpoints or hurdles to be cleared; they are integral, ongoing processes that bolster the integrity and efficacy of an organization's security measures. By adopting a proactive and integrated approach to audits, utilizing advanced tools for reporting and remediation, and embracing the potential of compliance as code, organizations can forge a security architecture that not only withstands scrutiny but also advances business objectives in a secure, compliant manner.

Incident Response

Incident response (IR) is a vital component of enterprise security architecture, serving as a structured methodology to manage and mitigate the aftermath of security incidents. An effective incident response strategy can significantly reduce the potential damage of breaches and expedite recovery times, thus maintaining business continuity and safeguarding an organization's reputation.

IR Frameworks

Various frameworks provide guidelines for establishing a robust incident response capability:

NIST SP 800-61

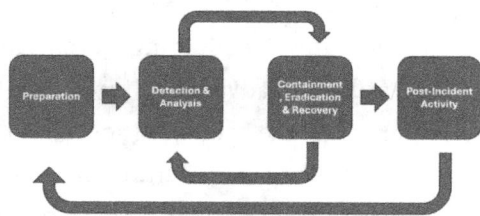

The National Institute of Standards and Technology's Special Publication 800-61 is a comprehensive guide for computer security incident handling. This framework emphasizes four phases: preparation, detection and analysis, containment eradication and recovery, and post-incident activity. Its key strength lies in its thorough approach to preparation, recommending organizations to have a formal incident response policy and plan, specific roles and communication strategies, and necessary resources and training to handle incidents effectively.

ISO/IEC 27035

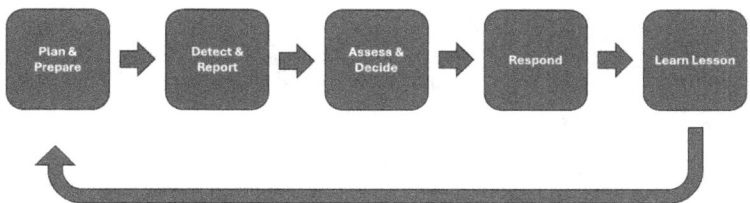

The International Organization for Standardization (ISO) and the International Electrotechnical Commission (IEC) have developed the ISO/IEC 27035 standard for incident management. This standard provides a structured and planned approach to: detect, report, and assess information security incidents; respond to and manage information security incidents and vulnerabilities; and improve the organization's information security through the continual learning and experience gained from managing information security incidents.

SANS Institute

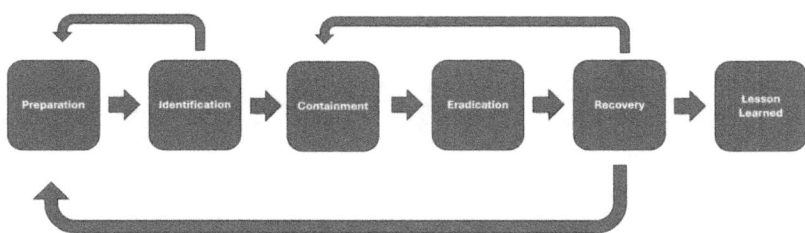

The SANS Institute, a highly regarded educational organization for cybersecurity professionals, has developed a widely recognized incident response framework that serves as a benchmark for handling security incidents effectively. The SANS framework emphasizes continuous improvement, with the lessons learned from past incidents informing ongoing refinements to the preparation phase. This cyclical nature ensures that incident response processes evolve in line with emerging threats and organizational changes.

Each of these frameworks brings a different emphasis to incident response, from NIST's structured process approach and ISO's standards for a systematic response to SANS Institute's practical security practices. In implementing an incident response strategy, organizations often adapt elements from multiple frameworks to suit their specific needs, industry requirements, and regulatory obligations.

A robust incident response capability embedded within an enterprise security architecture is vital. It requires not only technical tools and processes but also strong leadership, cross-departmental collaboration, and clear communication channels. By drawing on established IR frameworks and customizing them to the context of their operations, organizations can create resilient and responsive incident response strategies that minimize the impact of security incidents and support rapid recovery.

Architecture Documentation

Cybersecurity architecture documentation is the meticulous recording and detailing of the structure and behavior of an organization's cybersecurity systems. This documentation is critical for several reasons:

Knowledge Sharing and Continuity: Documentation ensures that knowledge about the cybersecurity architecture is not tacit but rather recorded and accessible. This is vital for onboarding new staff, transitioning between teams, or ensuring business continuity in the face of personnel changes.

Strategic Planning and Analysis: Well-maintained documentation allows for thorough analysis of the current security posture and informed strategic planning. It helps in identifying areas of strength, as well as gaps and vulnerabilities that may require attention.

Compliance and Legal Requirements: Detailed documentation helps in demonstrating compliance with various industry standards and legal requirements. It provides evidence that security controls are in place and that the organization takes a structured approach to security.

Incident Response and Recovery: During security incidents, having comprehensive documentation can significantly expedite the response and recovery process by providing clear guidelines and reference points.

Maintenance and Troubleshooting: Regular operations and maintenance activities are facilitated by having accurate documentation that outlines the configuration and integration points of various security systems.

Architecture Views

The architecture should be captured from various perspectives, including:

Logical View: This includes the high-level overview of the security architecture, showcasing how various components such as firewalls, intrusion detection systems, and data encryption protocols fit together.

Physical View: The physical aspect documents the actual hardware and network infrastructure involved in the security architecture, including server layouts, network diagrams, and data center designs.

Data Flow View: This details how data moves through the system, outlining the controls in place at each step to ensure the data remains secure. It covers aspects like encryption at rest and in transit, access controls, and data integrity checks.

Environmental View: This perspective considers the external factors that impact the security architecture, such as regulatory requirements, third-party integrations, and the overall cyber threat landscape.

Artifacts produced as part of cybersecurity architecture documentation may include:

Architecture Diagrams: Visual representations of systems, data flows, and controls, which provide a clear picture of the security landscape. As much as possible, diagrams should use formal notation for ease of sharing across organizations and integration with architecture tools.

Threat Models: As covered in an earlier chapter, threat models systematically identify and document potential threats and vulnerabilities that could compromise the confidentiality, integrity, or availability of a system. This includes external threats such as malicious attacks from hackers, as well as internal risks such as unauthorized access or data leakage. Threat models document should also include recommended countermeasures and security controls to address identified threats and vulnerabilities. This includes technical controls such as encryption, access controls, and intrusion detection systems, as well as procedural measures such as security policies, training programs, and incident response plans.

Test Cases: Test cases validate the effectiveness and robustness of security controls and mitigation measures implemented within the system architecture. These test cases simulate real-world attack scenarios, including penetration testing, vulnerability scanning, and security assessments, to evaluate the system's resilience against known threats and attack vectors.

Policy Documents: Written policies that outline the governance of security practices, such as access control policies, incident response plans, and data protection policies.

Standard Operating Procedures (SOPs): Detailed procedures for routine operations, which ensure consistency and reliability in the implementation of security practices.

Audit Reports: Records of past audits, including findings, recommendations, and actions taken, which serve as a history of the security posture over time.

Compliance Checklists: Lists used to ensure that all necessary compliance measures are being followed and documented correctly.

Architecture Language

Using a formal language, like ArchiMate, for architecture documentation offers numerous advantages in capturing, communicating, and managing the complexities inherent in modern enterprise architectures.

Firstly, a formal language provides a structured framework with well-defined concepts, relationships, and syntax, ensuring consistency and clarity in documentation. This structured approach facilitates precise representation of architectural elements, their interconnections, and dependencies across different layers of the enterprise, ranging from business processes to technology infrastructure.

Secondly, formal languages enable effective communication among stakeholders with diverse backgrounds and perspectives, including business executives, IT professionals, architects, and developers. By adopting a common notation and vocabulary, it can foster shared understanding and alignment of architectural decisions and objectives, promoting collaboration and decision-making across organizational boundaries.

Thirdly, using a formal language facilitates analysis and evaluation of architecture documentation through automated tools and techniques. These tools support validation, simulation, and impact analysis, enabling architects to assess the implications of proposed changes, identify risks and bottlenecks, and optimize architectural designs more efficiently.

Furthermore, formal languages integrate with industry standards and best practices, enabling organizations to align architecture documentation with regulatory requirements, compliance frameworks, and recognized methodologies. By leveraging these standards, organizations can ensure governance, security, and scalability in their architectural practices, mitigating risks and enhancing overall performance.

Below is an example of a deployment diagram in informal notation vs. the same system documented in formal notation.

Informal Notation

Cybersecurity Architecture Fundamentals

Formal Notation

[Diagram showing deployment notation with Internet User PC, Admin User PC, Application Server (<<execution Environment>> :J2EE Server), and Database Server. Artifacts include App-client.jar and ServerApp.ear with <<deploy>> and <<artifact>> relationships, connected via Internet and Intranet.]

As you can see, the use of formal notation is preferred over informal diagrams for documenting systems due to several significant advantages:

Precision and Clarity: Formal notations provide precise and unambiguous representations of system components, relationships, and behaviors. Unlike informal diagrams, which may rely on vague or ambiguous symbols and annotations, formal notation ensures clear and consistent communication of architectural concepts and details. This precision reduces the risk of misinterpretation and misunderstanding among stakeholders, promoting effective decision-making and implementation.

Standardization: Formal notations adhere to standardized syntax, semantics, and modeling guidelines, ensuring consistency and interoperability across different documentation artifacts and architectural models. In contrast, informal diagrams may vary widely in style, structure, and content, making it challenging to integrate and compare information from multiple sources. Standardization facilitates collaboration, reuse, and maintenance of architectural documentation over time, particularly in complex and dynamic systems environments.

Analysis and Validation: Formal notations support automated analysis and validation techniques, enabling architects to perform rigorous assessments of system properties, constraints, and requirements. Tools and algorithms can analyze formal models for correctness, completeness, and consistency, detecting errors, conflicts, and inefficiencies that may go unnoticed in informal diagrams. This capability enhances the quality and reliability of architectural documentation, leading to more robust and resilient system designs.

Scalability and Complexity Management: Formal notations are better suited for representing complex systems and architectures, accommodating large-scale and intricate relationships among components, layers, and domains. Informal diagrams may struggle to capture the full extent of system complexity, leading to oversimplification or omission of critical details. Formal notation provides the expressive power and flexibility needed to model diverse aspects of architecture, from high-level strategic views to low-level implementation details, without sacrificing clarity or coherence.

Compliance and Governance: Formal notations facilitate alignment with industry standards, regulations, and best practices governing system development, deployment, and operation. By documenting architectures using recognized formal languages and frameworks, organizations can demonstrate compliance with relevant requirements, assess adherence to predefined guidelines, and manage risks associated with non-compliance. This alignment enhances transparency, accountability, and trust in architectural decision-making processes, especially in regulated industries or mission-critical systems environments.

In essence, cybersecurity architecture documentation is not merely a formality; it is a cornerstone of a robust security posture. It provides the blueprints that guide an organization in protecting its digital assets, ensuring operational effectiveness, and meeting compliance obligations. Without it, an organization's defenses may become disjointed and reactive rather than cohesive and proactive.

Documenting a View

Documenting an architecture view is a multifaceted process that captures the various dimensions of an enterprise's cybersecurity framework. A comprehensive documentation approach encompasses several critical components, each serving to enhance the clarity, utility, and robustness of the architectural blueprint.

At the forefront is the **primary presentation**, a graphical depiction of the architecture that illustrates the interconnections and relationships between different elements within the system. It serves as a visual map, simplifying complex structures into an understandable format. To ensure the clarity of this visual guide, a key or legend is crucial. It deciphers the notation used, elucidates the meaning of each symbol, and aids stakeholders in navigating the architectural landscape effectively.

Supplementing the primary presentation is the **element catalog**. This catalog provides a detailed directory of the architecture's components listed in the graphical representation. Typically formatted as a table, it offers a textual description for each element, capturing its purpose, nature, and role within the larger system. The element catalog serves as a reference point for understanding each component's functionality and significance.

The **variability guide** is an instrumental part of the documentation that identifies the adaptable facets of the architecture where customization and configuration can occur. It addresses areas such as:

Number of Instances
Guidelines for scaling, specifying how many instances of a particular service or application can exist within a pool.

Component Inclusion

The conditions under which optional components, such as plug-ins or add-ons, should be integrated into the system.

Implementation Choices

Options for selecting between different implementations of a component or connector, based on performance, security, or compatibility considerations.

Parameterization

Protocols for setting parameterized values that can be adjusted at build, deployment, or runtime, providing flexibility and customization for the architecture.

Architecture Background

This narrative component delves into the reasoning behind design decisions, shedding light on why certain paths were chosen over others. It documents the outcomes of various analyses, prototyping efforts, and experiments that informed the design process. Furthermore, it lists all the underlying assumptions and constraints that could impact the architecture, providing context and justifying the selected architectural approach.

Related Views

A crucial aspect of documentation is the inclusion of related views, which serve to contextualize the architecture within the broader framework. These references could point to higher-level parent views that give an overarching perspective of the system or to detailed child views that focus on specific subsystems or components.

The act of documenting an architecture view is not merely a technical necessity but a strategic asset. It encapsulates the collective cybersecurity wisdom of an organization, offering a tangible reference that guides current operations and informs future evolution. It ensures that the security architecture is not only understood but is also effectively communicated, managed, and optimized over time.

Architecture Decisions Document (ADD)

When you make key decision regarding the architecture design, it is necessary to communicate why certain decisions were made. A good way to do this is by creating a series of architecture decision documents.

An Architecture Decision Document is a formal record of the design decisions made during the development and maintenance of an architecture. This document is pivotal in capturing the rationale behind certain architectural choices and ensuring that these decisions are communicated clearly among all stakeholders. Here's a breakdown of what the ADD should contain:

Subject Area: The subject area provides a succinct description of the scope of the architecture decision. It acts as the title for the decision and should be specific enough to differentiate it from other decisions.

Design Decision: This section outlines the actual choice that has been made regarding the architectural approach or component. It describes what is being agreed upon and should be clear and concise.

Issues or Problem Statement: This is a detailed description of the problem or challenge that the design decision aims to address. It lays out the context and specific issues that necessitate a decision, outlining any technical constraints, business requirements, or user needs that are relevant.

Assumptions: Here, all the assumptions that have been made in the context of the decision are documented. Assumptions could be related to technology, business strategies, market trends, or user behavior. It's essential to identify these assumptions explicitly, as they form the foundation upon which the decision is based.

Motivation: The motivation section delves into the reasons why the decision is important. It explains the benefits expected from making this decision, how it aligns with broader business objectives, or its role in addressing technical challenges.

Alternatives: A list and description of alternative options that were considered before arriving at the current decision. This section demonstrates that different approaches were evaluated and provides a comparison basis.

Decision: This section succinctly states the chosen path or solution among the alternatives. It is the conclusive part that indicates the preferred option moving forward.

Justification: Justification provides the reasoning behind the chosen decision. It includes an analysis of how the decision addresses the issues or problem statement, why it stands out among the alternatives, and the benefits it provides over other options.

Implication: Here, the potential impacts of the decision are discussed. This may include changes to workflows, additional costs, shifts in timelines, or impacts on other architectural components. Understanding the implications is crucial for planning and for anticipating any downstream effects of the decision.

Related Decisions: Often, one architectural decision will influence or be influenced by other decisions. This section documents those relationships and helps to provide a holistic view of the interconnected nature of architectural decisions.

An Architecture Decision Document is an essential tool in the governance of enterprise architecture. It ensures that each decision is made with consideration of its wider impacts, aligns with the enterprise's strategic direction, and is made transparent to all members of the organization. By meticulously documenting decisions, enterprises can maintain a clear record that supports consistent and coherent architectural growth and change management over time.

Examples of an ADD

Section	Description	Example
Subject Area	What is it related to	Authentication
Design Decision	What is the decision you have to make	Use Facebook ID, other social media login or internal ID
Issue or Problem Statement	Explain why a choice has to be made	Unsure how many users have Facebook account How to manage and verify local ID
Assumption	List assumptions made when making decision	80% of the target customers have Facebook accounts Facebook does a better job at ID verification than the internal team
Motivation	What drives the decision	Ensure minimal steps for customer to create login
Alternatives	List all other options you have considered	Google ID Apple ID
Decision	What was the decision made	Use Facebook ID
Justification	Explain Decision	Developer only knows Facebook API
Implication	Explain any side effect	Customer who avoid having a Facebook account will not come to your site
Related Decision	List other decision that are related	Decision #2 – User Verification process

Putting It All Together

Congratulations on completing your journey through the fundamentals of enterprise cybersecurity architecture. Throughout this book, we have explored the essential components and principles that underpin a robust cybersecurity architecture, from understanding threat models to selecting appropriate technologies and documenting architecture decisions. Now, as we conclude, let's bring all these pieces together to create a comprehensive cybersecurity framework that protects your organization against a myriad of threats.

Integration of Threat Models

At the heart of every effective cybersecurity architecture lies a deep understanding of potential threats. By integrating threat models into our architecture design, we can anticipate and mitigate risks proactively. Begin by revisiting your threat models, ensuring they accurately reflect the current threat landscape and your organization's specific vulnerabilities. Identify potential attack vectors, such as unauthorized access, data breaches, or malware infiltration, and prioritize them based on their likelihood and potential impact.

Technology Selection

Selecting the right technologies is crucial for building a resilient cybersecurity architecture. Consider a multi-layered approach, incorporating a combination of preventative, detective, and responsive measures. Evaluate available technologies based on their ability to address identified threats and align with your organization's security objectives and infrastructure requirements. Whether it's firewalls, intrusion detection systems, encryption protocols, or advanced endpoint protection, each technology should complement others to create a cohesive defense strategy.

Architecture Diagrams in All Views

Visualizing your cybersecurity architecture through comprehensive diagrams is essential for understanding its intricacies and communicating effectively with stakeholders. Create architecture diagrams that illustrate different views of your security infrastructure, including network topology, data flow, access controls, and incident response procedures. These diagrams should not only capture the current state of your architecture but also allow for scalability and adaptability to future threats and technological advancements.

Architecture Decision Documents

Documenting architecture decisions ensures clarity, transparency, and accountability throughout the design and implementation process. Create detailed architecture decision documents (ADDs) that outline the rationale behind each decision, including technology selection, risk assessments, and trade-offs. These documents serve as valuable references for future iterations of your cybersecurity architecture and provide insights for audits, compliance requirements, and stakeholder reviews.

As you conclude the development of your enterprise cybersecurity architecture, remember that it's an ongoing journey rather than a finite destination. Continuously monitor and evaluate your architecture against emerging threats, evolving technologies, and organizational changes. Regularly update your threat models, revisit technology choices, and refine architecture documentation to ensure your defenses remain robust and resilient.

By integrating threat models, carefully selecting technologies, creating comprehensive architecture diagrams, and documenting architecture decisions, you'll establish a solid foundation for safeguarding your organization's digital assets. With diligence, collaboration, and a commitment to cybersecurity best practices, you can navigate the ever-changing landscape of cyber threats and protect your enterprise from harm.

About the Author
Ian Loe

https://ianloe.com

Ian has more than 27 years of experience in the IT industry with wide industry experience spanning public sector to financial services. He has deep knowledge in both infrastructure and application security with deep expertise in governance and security technologies.

Ian has served as CIO, CTO & CISO in large conglomerates and have deep experience in managing cybersecurity, infrastructure, architecture & data engineering for various organisations. Ian has introduced many modern approaches to technology management including implementing Hyper Converged Infrastructure (HCI), DevSecOps, FinOps, SRE, Risk Based Management, and the use of Breach & Attack Simulation (BAS) platforms.

He has held other senior appointments such as Director, Government Cybersecurity Operations and was responsible for managing cybersecurity operations for the whole of government in Singapore, which includes the monitoring of and response to cybersecurity incidents. He is also an regular industry speaker on many topics and an active adjunct.

www.ingramcontent.com/pod-product-compliance
Lightning Source LLC
Chambersburg PA
CBHW052151220526
45471CB00004B/1627